DANIEL SUHR
A STORY OF SEPTEMBER 11ᵀᴴ

Paul Conlon

TWIN MOUNTAIN PRESS

To the 343 and counting.

CONTENTS

That's the way it is. Good days. And bad days. Up days. Down days. Sad days. Happy days. But never a boring day on this job. You do what God has called you to do. You show up. You put one foot in front of another. You get on the rig and you go out and you do the job—which is a mystery. And a surprise. You have no idea when you get on that rig. No matter how big the call. No matter how small. You have no idea what God is calling you to. But he needs you. He needs me. He needs all of us.

FDNY Chaplain Father Mychal Judge
From his last homily on September 10, 2001
at Engine Company 73 and Ladder Company 42

Chapter 1

MONDAY 9-17-01

DANIEL SUHR was the first firefighter to perish on September 11, 2001. His funeral was held the following Monday at 10:00 AM in St. Edmunds Roman Catholic Church in Brooklyn. Later that same day I was standing with a group of firefighters on the corner of West Street and Liberty Street. The devastation was overwhelming. The destruction complete. For the past week most members of the FDNY had spent more time here than at home, but none of them could get used to this place—the site that had come to be known as The Pile. A mountain of debris rose slowly and steadily to the north and east, punctuated by a ten-story section of the south wall of the south tower that was still standing.

Another section of wall, maybe one hundred feet long by fifty feet high, stood on West Street. At first glance it might appear that this had been the western boundary of one of the towers, but then it became clear. This was a section of wall that broke off and fell from some sickening height and landed with such force that it became impaled in the street. It was surrounded by twisted steel and concrete and dust.

Twisted Steel. They are just words, unless you stop for a moment and think about it. A structural engineer will tell you that the strength of a beam—its load bearing capacity—is directly related to its depth.

1

The World Trade Center had an unusual design, basically a tube within a tube. Steel box beams, fourteen inches square, were used to form the exterior walls. They were spaced closely together, sixty on a side, each face of each building two hundred and nine feet long. In effect, the exterior of the building was a beam, a two hundred and nine foot square beam, the depth of which gave it tremendous resistance to lateral loads. Those box beams rose one hundred and ten stories into the sky and now they lay interlocked and deformed and twisted.

In addition, each building had a center core constructed with massive steel columns, some nearly two feet by four feet, with a finished length over 1000 feet. They rose from bedrock to just below roof level and were heavily braced and interconnected their entire height. The center core was one hundred and thirty feet long and eighty-eight feet wide. Within it was the elevators and stairs and utilities. The center core was constructed to resist the forces of gravity while the perimeter columns resisted the forces of both gravity and wind. Web joists were connected to the center core and the outer columns at each story. The web joists were two and a half feet from top to bottom chord with steel decking welded to the top and concrete poured on the steel decking to form the floors. The concrete and steel acted in combination to create stiff bracing, securing the center core to the exterior walls.

When the planes hit, they destroyed numerous exterior columns on several floors, from the 93rd to 99th floor in the north tower and from the 77th to 85th floor in the south. They dumped their jet fuel onto the concrete floors and the fuel ignited and heated the columns that remained. The heat caused the columns to soften and bend and the burning fuel also weakened the anchor clips that fastened the web joists to the columns.

Eventually the columns buckled and the clips failed and the most seriously damaged floor could no longer support the load imposed by the floors above it and it gave way. The floors fell onto the floor below.

The floor below was not designed for such a massive impact load and so that floor failed and fell. Then each successive floor failed and the entire structure collapsed onto itself. The towers that had taken eight years to plan and four years to build now suffered a complete and catastrophic collapse in just over ten seconds.

Each building weighed over 500,000 tons. As they plowed into the earth massive compressive forces were generated and vast amounts of energy released. The debris field consisted of concrete and twisted steel and dust—so much dust. But where was everything else? Where were the desks and computers and file cabinets? Where were the chairs and closets and copy machines? Where were the mops and buckets, the slop sinks and faucets? Where were the office partitions with bulletin boards attached and family photos held in place by pushpins? Where were the doors? Over 40,000 doors were installed when the buildings went up, and 3,000 miles of electrical wire, and 43,000 windows. There was only concrete, and twisted steel, and dust.

And where were the people? Where were all those poor souls who were missing? The receptionists and dishwashers and carpenters, the bankers and lawyers and electricians, the elevator mechanics and Port Authority police officers, the janitors and Wall Street traders? Where were the hundreds of firefighters, and NYPD police officers? And what about the tourists—the people from all over the United States, from Asia and Africa and Europe? From South America and Australia?

It was getting late. The sun was setting and the sky was growing dark. One by one, clusters of powerful electric lights came on, flooding the scene in an artificial glare. Soon the site was starkly lit, but the sky was still growing dark, progressively darker from east to west, and the bright lights made the darkness just outside the site seem that much deeper. Smoke rose from numerous fires roaring deep within the pile, and the rising smoke was illuminated by the lights. An insidious odor permeated everything. The odor mingled with the smoke, but was separate from it, distinctive and malevolent. The odor would soon become inexorably linked with Ground Zero.

The humming, pounding sound of diesel engines was constant. The diesel engines powered fire engines and tower ladders, backhoes, grapplers and dump trucks, and they powered the electric lights. The diesel exhaust hung in the air. The fire engines supplied water to hose lines that ran throughout the site and they supplied the tower ladders that poured water on the fires. Bucket brigades snaked up and down the peaks and valleys formed by the hundreds of thousands of tons of debris. The members of the bucket brigades worked ceaselessly trying to remove the debris by hand. Firefighters scrambled deeper and deeper onto the pile and lower and lower into the subbasements and foundation, spelunking through the maze of destruction, searching for survivors.

Survivors. None had been found since that past Wednesday at 1:30 PM when Genelle Guzman-McMillan was rescued—the last victim found alive. She was one of only eighteen people who survived the collapse of the north tower; no one survived the collapse of the south tower. Yet sixteen firefighters had been ordered into the building just moments before it collapsed, and thirteen of them, including myself, are still alive. This is the story of Daniel Suhr, the firefighter who saved us.

Chapter 2
HOMECREST

In 1964 the Beatles arrived in America and the Verrazano Narrows Bridge opened. That same year the first Ford Mustang came off the assembly line in Detroit, Bob Dylan released *The Times They Are a-Changin'* and Cassius Clay beat Sonny Liston in the Heavyweight Boxing Championship of the World. This was the year that Martin Luther King was awarded the Nobel Peace Prize, New York City hosted the World's Fair in Flushing Meadows Park, Lyndon Johnson signed the Civil Rights Act into law, and Congress passed the Gulf of Tonkin Resolution, which led to American involvement in Vietnam. It was also the year that final plans for a brand new World Trade Center in lower Manhattan were approved. But for Ed and Sheila Suhr the big news in 1964 was that on Friday, August 21st their third child, Daniel, was born.

Ed and Sheila Suhr lived in a two-family house on 19th Street between Avenue R and Avenue S in the Homecrest section of Brooklyn. They purchased their home with another couple, life-long friends, whom they eventually bought out in the 1970's. They went on to have six children—two daughters and four sons: Jean, Ed, Daniel, Lee, Chris and James. It was a good neighborhood, a working class neighborhood, with Kelly Park nearby and grocery stores, bakeries, and bars all within walking distance.

Sheila set high standards for her children, and yet if they failed, as long as they kept trying, she was patient and merciful. She was tough yet fair, demanding yet loving, and she raised six children, all respectful and self-reliant. Daniel's father Ed had become a firefighter in 1960 and would protect the citizens of New York for thirty-four years. He was first assigned to Engine Company 323 in Old Mill Basin and then Engine Company 254 in Homecrest. Like most firefighters, he worked second jobs to pay the bills—hanging sheet rock, spackling and painting.

Daniel's brother Chris said, "All my father did was work. And he was never the same after Dan's death." Ed Suhr suffered a heart attack in November 2001 while on a hunting trip with Chris and a few friends. He underwent quadruple bypass surgery and lived three more years, passing away in September of 2004. When Ed Suhr was suffering chest pains in the hunting cabin in upstate New York he told Chris not to bother with an ambulance, not to make a big deal out of it, that he would be all right. Chris got an ambulance anyway and when he called his mother at two o'clock in the morning from the hospital where his father had been transported, she answered the phone very simply, true to her no-nonsense, caring character, "Who's hurt? And how bad is it?"

The Suhr children went to St. Edmund's Elementary School and then the sisters went to Edward R. Murrow High School and the brothers went to James Madison. Daniel started playing football at the age of six, for the Brooklyn Hurricanes, first as a Pee Wee. At James Madison High School he was All-City as a sophomore, junior and senior. He played one year at both the State University of New York at Albany and at the College of the Desert in Palm Desert, California, just outside of Palm Springs. He joined the Brooklyn Mariners, a semi-pro team, when he was nineteen and he played for the FDNY football team, The Bravest, as soon as he was allowed to play after getting on the Fire Department in 1985. He was a middle linebacker and played some tight end. He was smart, aggressive and big; he played with one hundred percent effort every second that he was on the field. He also played baseball in high school, but football was his passion.

High school can be a tough place, but Daniel would always take the time to stop and to smile and to say hello, especially to the kids who felt left out. Daniel always said, "It doesn't hurt to smile" and "Give people a smile" and "What does it cost to smile?" Chris Suhr was always amazed at how Daniel would engage those kids who needed it most, how kind and compassionate he was. Daniel took the time to notice people, especially those who are easy to ignore.

Chris related a story about one of Daniel's first days at the College of the Desert. He went to the college with hopes of playing linebacker and while playing a game of touch football with some friends on campus, an older man approached. The man began talking to Daniel and his friends, he was taking his time, choosing his words carefully, and soon the others grew tired of listening and one by one went back to their game, all except Daniel. Even though it seemed the man had nothing to offer, Daniel did what he always did. He looked him in the eye and smiled. He treated him with respect.

At last, the man revealed who he was—a millionaire, a very influential member of the community, and a football coach at the college. He was a good man to know, especially if you were a new football player at a new school. The man offered to take Daniel out to dinner, and Daniel asked if his friends could come along. The man instantly liked Daniel and soon they became close. The man started to take Daniel out for breakfast on Sundays, became his mentor, and guided his progress as a college football player. This was how Daniel Suhr lived, he treated those around him well, with dignity, and his character had a positive effect on everyone he met.

• • •

Nancy Lanzetta was born in 1965, one of four children. She had two older sisters, Luanne and Donna, and a younger brother, Neil. Her parents, Nancy and Louis, owned a two-family home on Avenue T between East 7th Street and East 8th Street in the Homecrest section of Brooklyn. They always rented out one of the apartments in the house to help meet their expenses. Louis was a police officer in the NYPD and he also had a sewer cleaning business on the side to earn extra income.

Daniel first asked Nancy out on March 2, 1978, when she was in seventh grade at St. Edmund's Elementary School and he was in eighth. Nancy went to St Edmunds High School but attended many of Daniel's football games at James Madison. As a sophomore he played offense and wore number 60. Soon enough he switched to defense, middle linebacker, and was given the number 90, the number he would wear for the rest of his life. Daniel was quick, and he hit hard. He anticipated where the play was going, had great football sense, and was tough to fool. Nancy loved watching him, how he tracked the ball and always made a play. The summer after he graduated from high school, he worked for Nancy's father in the sewer cleaning business. As Daniel joked, the work was shitty, but the money was good.

He worked for Louis again the summer between Albany and the College of the Desert. Louis loved him like a son and recognized that Daniel was going to need money at school. Instead of paying him his full salary each week, he set some money aside. In August when Daniel was ready to leave, Louis gave him the rest of the money he had earned. After transferring to the College of the Desert, Nancy wasn't crazy about him going all the way to California for school, and Daniel's mother didn't like it either. But Daniel wanted to play football there in the hopes of being scouted and picked up by a big college program.

Things started off well for Daniel at the College of the Desert. He was starting at middle linebacker and playing hard. But then he dislocated his shoulder. He practiced day after day and he played week after week, but was never one hundred percent. He played through the pain, and he played well, well enough to be named All-Conference. But still, he wasn't signed by any of the elite schools. He was also living a different lifestyle than he had been used to and never really settled in. After a year he decided to come home.

When he got home he started playing for the Brooklyn Mariners. The coach was an FDNY firefighter, Pudgy Walsh. Pudgy also ran a class in Brooklyn to prepare candidates for the physical portion of the firefighters entrance exam. Daniel signed up for the prep class and dedicated himself to it, just as he had on the football field. When he took the Fire Department test he got a 100 on the physical and scored a 99 on the written. He was at the top of the list. Actually, he scored so well that when his number was reached, he was too young to accept it. The FDNY requires firefighters to be at least 21 years old. So Daniel had to wait for the next class when he was old enough. He was appointed to the FDNY on October 7, 1985.

Daniel loved becoming a firefighter, he was absolutely ecstatic, overjoyed. He couldn't believe that he would make a living doing what he considered to be the best job in the world. At the fire academy, or Proby School as it is known in the fire department, he excelled at the physical aspects of the training: raising ladders; forcing doors; moving hose lines; rappelling off buildings; push-ups, sit-ups, running, and the rest. But he wasn't too enthusiastic about the classroom work. He was also juggling the demands of Proby School with spending time at Nancy's and visiting his older brother, Ed. Ed was in a rehab facility in the Bronx. He had graduated from West Point in June of 1984 and was involved in a nearly fatal car accident three months later. September was a terrible month for the Suhr family.

Nancy was proud of Daniel, and because Daniel was extremely happy to be a firefighter, she was happy too. When Daniel graduated from the fire academy, he was assigned to Engine Company 216 on

Union Avenue in the Williamsburg section of Brooklyn. This was a busy firehouse with a good reputation. It was the firehouse where his coach on the Brooklyn Mariners, Pudgy Walsh, had worked as a firefighter. By the time Daniel was assigned to Engine 216 Pudgy had been promoted to lieutenant and was working elsewhere but he knew Daniel's character, his work habits, his intelligence, his strength. Pudgy requested that he be assigned to his old firehouse, and Daniel Suhr spent the next sixteen years as a firefighter in Engine Company 216.

Chapter 3
MONDAY 9-10-01

ENGINE COMPANY 216 sits on a busy section of Union Avenue. The El train passes the firehouse just down the block on Broadway and the NYPD 90 Precinct Station House adjoins it. Engine Company 216 shares the firehouse with Ladder Company 108 and Battalion 35. These Companies have a long history of service, with Engine 216 and Ladder 108 predating the formation of New York City itself.

Engine Company 216 was first established as Engine 16 on September 15, 1872 in the Brooklyn Fire Department, or BFD. It replaced Volunteer Hose Company No. 6 on Stagg Street near Union Avenue. By 1893 the company moved to a brand new firehouse at 11 Scholes Street. On January 1, 1898 New York City was consolidated and Brooklyn was no longer a separate city, therefore on January 28, 1898 Engine 16 officially became a part of the FDNY. It was renumbered 15 years later on October 1st and became Engine 216. The company moved to its present home at 187 Union Avenue on October 13, 1971. Engine Company 216 has been protecting the citizens of Williamsburg for 150 years.

Similarly, Ladder 108 began as BFD Ladder 8, became part of the FDNY in 1898, was renumbered to Ladder 58 the next year and to Ladder 108 14 years later. They moved from 112 Siegel Street to the new quarters at 187 Union Avenue on August 9, 1971. Battalion 35 was organized on April 15, 1906, moved into the firehouse on Seigel Street with Ladder 108 in 1927 and then to Union Avenue with Ladder 108.

Many exceptional, dedicated firefighters have worked in these companies since the very beginning. They have time-honored traditions and have responded to countless fires and emergencies through the years. On January 14, 1880 Engine 16 responded to a fire in the Otto Huber Brewery in Williamsburg. The Captain of Engine 16, William Baldwin, was struck when the walls of the brewery collapsed. He died of his injuries six days later, the first member of the Brooklyn Fire Department to die in the line of duty.

· · ·

In the FDNY the day is broken up into two tours: the 9x6 tour and the 6x9 tour, or the day tour and the night tour. The day tour is from 9:00AM to 6:00PM and the night tour from 6:00PM to 9:00AM. At the beginning of each tour the members gather for roll call. Roll call is conducted to determine assignments and to discuss scheduled activities, to review recent operations and be alerted to hazardous conditions. At roll call information is exchanged, both important and trivial. And so on Monday September 10, 2001, at 9:00 AM, four firefighters and an officer stood in front of Engine Company 216 on the apparatus floor of the firehouse on Union Avenue in Brooklyn.

I was a covering officer, as it is known in the FDNY, filling in for the tour. I had been promoted to captain just two days prior and had nineteen years on the job, but had worked in Manhattan and the Bronx, not Brooklyn, and had never worked in this firehouse. Covering officer's work in companies all over the city and have no way of knowing every firefighter in every firehouse on the job. They don't know the regular captain's policy regarding riding positions or the traditions of each firehouse, so they often seek out a senior firefighter in the company to help give the proper assignments. Even before I asked, one firefighter standing in front of the rig, Daniel Suhr, offered to help. Daniel was a large man, with an open, honest face, and he advised me as to the best assignments for the members working. This is what good firefighters in good firehouses do.

Daniel Suhr introduced Firefighter Bill Whelan. Bill had short white hair, bright blue eyes and an Irish brogue. He had more time on the job than anyone else in the Company and was one of the four regular chauffeurs in Engine 216. In engine companies the chauffeur is the firefighter who drives the apparatus and supplies water for the fire. They find a working hydrant, connect a hose line from the hydrant to the rig, operate the pumps, set the proper volume and pressure, and supply water to hose lines stretched from their pumper to extinguish the fire. Bill Whelan was also the president of the Emerald Society of the FDNY, a fraternal organization for firefighters of Irish heritage. Bill Whelan would, of course, be the chauffeur for the tour. Daniel Suhr advised that Firefighter Lagan could take the nozzle, the "pipe" as he called it, Firefighter Braunreuther the control position, the "hook-up", and Daniel would be the back-up Firefighter.

Engine 216 was scheduled for Building Inspection that morning, so I took the next four or five Building Record Cards from the file cabinet in the company office. When we arrived at the first address Daniel Suhr asked if he might look at the cards. I handed them to him and after glancing at them he looked up, shaking his head, smiling as he spoke, "You got to be kidding me. *These* buildings?"

"They were next one's on the list," I said.

"You'll be writing reports all day," he said. He held the cards tight and they looked especially small in his hand.

"We'll do one, see how it goes."

"We got some big, beautiful, brand new buildings a few blocks from here," he said. He gestured with his arm and pointed with the cards. I was smiling now, and the other firefighters too, and he handed the cards back to me. We wound up inspecting the buildings anyway and wrote a few violations and referrals to other city agencies. But it was perfectly clear that Daniel was just looking out for the covering officer.

Engine 216 had a few runs during Building Inspection: an elderly man who was having difficulty breathing, a car accident, a gas leak and a false alarm. We returned to the firehouse around 1:00 PM and the firefighters from Ladder 108 had prepared lunch. After lunch I wanted to conduct a company drill, to share some information on fires in Project-Type buildings. Projects are high-rise fireproof multiple dwellings. I had noticed that there were several Projects in the area, and since Engine 216 and Ladder 108 had been busy units for many years, they would have learned valuable lessons fighting fires in these types of buildings. Although firefighting procedures were standardized throughout the Fire Department, each borough faced different challenges and most neighborhoods had unique fire problems. Many firehouses developed ingenious solutions to the particular problems they faced.

One of the beauties of the job was that covering officers were exposed to a wide range of experience as they traveled throughout the city. And one of the hallmarks of the Department was that everyone constantly shared any and all information that might help other firefighters do the job a little more safely or efficiently. The result was an environment created that was beneficial to all—the firefighters and the citizens we served. Covering officers were in the unique position of being able to take what they learned from each company in which they worked and share it with any other firehouses in the future.

I let the firefighters know that I wanted to give a drill. And even though the members of Engine 216 had other work to do, even though they had been out of the firehouse all day, once they cleaned up from lunch, Daniel Suhr was the first to sit at one of the two large rectangular tables in the kitchen and wait for the drill to begin. The other members of the company followed his lead.

In New York City, buildings over 75 feet are considered high-rise buildings. To deliver water to fight fires on the upper floors, these buildings are equipped with standpipes. Standpipes run from the ground floor to the roof, with a siamese connection at street level and outlets on each floor. The engine company chauffeur attaches a hose line from the pumper to the siamese connection to supply water to the standpipe so that water is available on every floor of the building. Firefighters can then attach hose lines to an outlet, usually on the floor below the fire, and stretch the hose to the fire area and extinguish the fire.

It requires coordination and planning in order to operate safely and efficiently in high-rise residential buildings, including the Projects in the response area of Engine Company 216 and Ladder Company 108. We sat at one of the tables in the kitchen and discussed supplying standpipes, hose line placement, past fires, potential problems and possible solutions. Daniel and Bill Whalen had especially good insight into some of the challenges they had faced in the past. It was a good drill, short and informative. Once we were done, I was about to leave the kitchen when Daniel Suhr picked up a pot of coffee. "Ready for some coffee, Cap?" Daniel asked. He held the pot in one hand and began reaching for a cup with the other. He looked me in the eye as he spoke, like he had all the time in the world.

"No. But thank you," I said. And I repeated thank you. I repeated it to express my appreciation for everything that Daniel had done in those first few hours since the day began. "Thank you."

At around three in the afternoon Engine Company 216 was assigned as the fourth due engine company to a fire on the second floor of a three-story wood frame dwelling on Metropolitan Avenue. The fire was confined to one room and was quickly extinguished. The firefighters began to repack their hoses and place the ladders and tools back on the rigs.

As the operation was ending it seemed that each of the 50 or so firefighters at the scene personally approached Daniel Suhr to exchange a few words with him, to share a quick story, to enjoy a few laughs. Once all the equipment was safely stowed a sudden downpour began. Large, fat drops of rain fell straight out of the low gray clouds, pounding the parked cars and chasing most of the firefighters back inside their rigs. Once I was inside the cab of Engine 216, Bill Whelan, sitting behind the steering wheel, smiled and motioned with his head and I followed his gaze. Daniel had not run out of the rain. He stood in the street, the raindrops splashing off the black asphalt around him, and looked intently at the firefighter who stood toe to toe with him. The rain pelted them on their helmets and turnout coats and boots. Daniel was nodding his head and gesturing with his arms, he seemed to be answering a question, giving some advice, and a blinding deluge wasn't going to stop him from helping a friend.

When we got back to the firehouse, Division 11 called with my assignment for the next day. I could have been told to report to any company in the city, but I was ordered back to Engine 216. And I was glad that I would return. I liked the firehouse and the firefighters, as well as the area they protected, or the little bit of it I had seen. I could leave my gear there for the night and not have to drag it back home. When covering officers work in a different firehouse each day, they need to take a quick look around, to get the layout and determine where everything is located, from the company office to the kitchen, from the bathroom to the nearest pole to slide down to the apparatus floor. Where is the Office Record Journal? Where are the forms that are required to get a tool repaired or replaced?

I looked in the daybook on the desk and saw that Daniel Suhr would also be working the next day, and I was happy about that. The most important job of a company officer at a fire or emergency is to accomplish the assigned mission, and to keep each firefighter safe while doing it. The officer is responsible for the four or five firefighters working that tour, for getting them back home in the same condition they were in when they arrived, and responsible for getting the job done in order to protect the lives and property of the citizens of New York. "Risk a little to save a little, Risk a lot to save a lot". Once you know the capabilities of the firefighters working on any given tour, the job of keeping them safe becomes more manageable. Even after working with him for just one tour I knew that Daniel was a knowledgeable, dedicated and experienced firefighter, a good man. It was obvious. He stood out among the outstanding firefighters of Engine 216 and Ladder 108, so I was glad that we would be working together again on the next day—Tuesday, September 11th.

Chapter 4

IMPACT

ON THE morning of September 11, 2001 the air was cool, and the sky was crystal clear. As I drove west on Metropolitan Avenue, the industrial borderline of Queens gave way to the three-story residential buildings of Brooklyn, and the World Trade Center came into view. This was, of course, not unusual; the twin towers could be seen all over New York City. But the way they stood out in the cloudless blue sky, in contrast to the older wood frame dwellings along Metropolitan Avenue, made me feel a little like a tourist 'taking in the view.'

Construction began on the World Trade Center in the late sixties, with the north tower completed in 1972 and the south tower in 1973. It was designed to reestablish New York City as a major center of world trade. A sixteen-acre superblock was created, with Vesey Street to the north, Church Street to the east, Liberty Street to the south and West Street to the west. Thirteen city blocks were eliminated, five through streets closed and an area known as Radio Row was razed in order to create the site.

In the 1960's Radio Row was a vibrant neighborhood. It was congested with small stores selling radios, TV's and telephones, record players and washers and dryers, dishwashers and refrigerators. The stores also sold spare parts to repair the appliances. They were filled floor to ceiling with condensers, tubes and potentiometers, with dials, capacitors and fuses, with bulbs and knobs, with soldering guns and switches. The sidewalks were crowded with people searching for the particular part, the tube or capacitor or switch, to make their radio work again and the narrow streets were jammed with cars. The sound of car horns and of music coming from the radios filled the air.

The first store on Radio Row had opened in the early 1920's and, over the next forty years, hundreds of businesses became part of this thriving community. When it was decided that the area would be subject to eminent domain and demolished, to make way for the World Trade Center, it felt so dense and established and necessary that it was hard to believe that it would all soon be gone. And it was inconceivable that in a short time the electronics of the twentieth century would become obsolete.

New Yorkers watched the twin towers rise, and when they were complete there was a consensus that they were unattractive, even ugly. They looked institutional, boring, bland. Yet, as the years passed the perception of them began to change. New Yorkers were captivated by the superlative nature of them, the size, the square footage. They were among the tallest buildings in the world. They used more electricity than Syracuse. They employed over 50,000 people, with 150,000 visitors each day, more than the population of many towns and cities across America; they had their own zip code. Felipe Petit humanized them. Terrorists had targeted them. Time had softened them. And now they had become a sort of touchstone, a landmark. City residents and visitors alike would look for them as they climbed the stairs out of a subway station or upon exiting a store, to get oriented at a glance; they anchored the southern tip of Manhattan. They became two more flawed characters in a city of flawed characters. And even though they weren't particularly appealing, they were a part of New York now.

• • •

I arrived at the firehouse in Williamsburg sometime before 8:00 AM, moved my gear from the rack in the rear to the front, next to Engine 216, and placed a bag of bagels on the counter in the kitchen. The firefighters in the kitchen drank coffee and fried eggs and read newspapers while talking and joking with one another. I said hello, poured a cup of coffee and headed up to the office on the second floor to relieve Lieutenant John Carver who had worked the 6x9 tour.

"How was your night?" I asked. He sat behind the large desk with his back to the wall.

"Not bad. A few runs after midnight."

"Anything going on today?"

"Well, you won't have Buildings again. I heard we kind of screwed you yesterday."

"Negative. Not at all."

"I didn't mean to leave you shit buildings to do."

"I know, John, really. I think they're just breaking your chops. We had a good day. I got to see some of the buildings; pick the guy's brains a bit. You know, Bill Whelan and Danny Suhr were working."

"Oh God, those two never stop talking," he said. And we smiled.

"I never worked in Brooklyn. It's all good," I said. John Carver got up and moved into the center of the room. I walked around him and sat down. The BF-4, or riding list, was on top of the desk. The BF-4 is a small rectangular form that officers' carry. It lists the members who are working on that particular tour, their assignments and riding positions. It was blank. John held on to the back of a wooden chair in front of the desk and leaned forward. We were exchanging information, changing roles, one of us was coming on duty and the other was getting off. And except for those firefighters who worked the 6x9 tour and were staying to work the 9x6, the same scenario was playing out all across

21

the city. Firefighters were relieving each other, catching up, exchanging information.

Lieutenant Carver continued, "You have a detail going to Engine 204. The proby's got the detail, John Johnson."

"Okay."

"There was a party last night, Bruce Foss retired, a good guy," Carver said. "If you need anything I'll be here for a while. I'll be downstairs."

He left the office to go down to the kitchen and join the others for a cup of coffee. He would soon change out of his uniform and go home. I glanced at the personal information sheet that every company maintained, facts about each member: name, date of birth, address, phone number, date of appointment to the Fire Department. The sheet sat beneath a rectangle of protective Plexiglas on top of the desk. I wanted to see how many years' experience each member working that day had. John Johnson was a probationary firefighter, a proby, with a year and a half on the job. He was actually assigned to Engine 302 in Queens but was on his "rotation" in Engine 216. The FDNY moved new firefighters into different firehouses during their first couple of years on the job, to allow for exposure to fire operations and to different firefighters throughout the city. Tony Sanseviro had eleven years in the Fire Department; Ted Murray and Chris Barry each had six, and Daniel Suhr had sixteen.

I began to fill out two copies of the riding list, a small square of carbon paper between each BF-4. The heading across the top of the form stated Company Number, Date, and Tour, I wrote E216, 9/11, and 9x6 in the appropriate spaces. I put my name on the top line of the first column on the left side of the form, and the designation 'Officer' next to it, on the top line of the second column. I also filled in the assignments for each member in the second column below Officer: Chauffeur; Nozzle; Back-Up; Control; Door. I didn't write the names of the firefighters beneath my name, next to their

22

assignments; I would take care of that at roll call. I put the two copies of the riding list in the left front pocket of my blue work shirt, or more accurately, my light blue shirt. As some firefighters liked to point out officers were "light blue collar" workers. They were supervisors, they didn't do the physical labor of firefighting, didn't even carry tools, not real tools, just a flashlight and a vestigial form of the Halligan known as a Sunilla tool.

I glanced at the papers in the outgoing basket, routine reports, and looked at the shelves of FDNY books on the wall behind the desk. Every office in every firehouse in the city had a similar collection of books and manuals. There were numerous thick volumes including Fire Codes and Laws; building construction; Hazardous Materials; Standard Operating Procedures for fires and emergencies in every type of structure in New York City; Subway Operations; Elevator Emergencies; Highway Operations; Utility Emergencies; Safety Bulletins; descriptions of recent unusual events; past issues of WNYF magazine; Administrative guides; Training Manuals; First Aid Manuals; tool lists; Fire Service Hydraulics; *Collapse of Burning Buildings* by Deputy Chief Vincent Dunne; Communication Manuals; Borough, Division and Battalion Directives and Circulars and numerous other books and resources.

There was a small metal box on the desk, next to a lamp, labeled "Emergency Notification Cards". It was painted green. Inside were index cards that contained the emergency contact information for each firefighter in the company: name; address; home phone number; name of spouse or significant other; phone number of the emergency contact; blood type; religion. This information was required to be updated every six months, in January and July of each year.

I was glad that Engine 216 had Building Inspection on Monday and therefore would not have it again that Tuesday, a "day off" as they joked about it in the firehouse. It was clear and cool out with low humidity, I knew one of the members working, it was my second tour as a captain, hell, I even knew where the bathroom was; it was starting to have the makings of a good day. Then again, as was also said in the firehouse, with a touch of gallows humor, it was the days that seemed like they might be uneventful that you had to watch out for. I left the office and walked down the stairs to the kitchen and wondered if I might know anyone else in the firehouse, maybe I had worked with one of the firefighters somewhere before, or a family member, or a mutual friend. One of the benefits of being a covering officer is meeting a lot of people. I poured a cup of coffee, sat down at one of the tables in the kitchen and buttered a bagel.

As I sat in the kitchen, John Johnson, the proby, was checking the rig. He turned on the valve of each air cylinder of every SCBA, Self-Contained Breathing Apparatus, or mask, that firefighters wear when in a contaminated environment. He checked the gauge to make sure there was enough air in the cylinder and to ensure the Vibralert activated. The Vibralert was designed to produce a high-pitched fluctuating alarm if a firefighter remained motionless for more than 20 seconds. He made sure each face piece of each mask was clean. He then checked the nozzles and hose and the compartment that held dozens of hose fittings. He checked the first aid equipment, the oxygen cylinders, oxygen masks, gloves, bandages, BP cuff and long-board. He dumped the stale water out of the large red cooler that was strapped to the side of the rig and refilled it with ice and fresh water. He strapped it back in place for the start of the new tour.

He wondered if they would "catch a job" today, Fire Department terminology for going to a fire. He had been to a few fires, and, like all probies, was anxious about going to the next one. He wanted to go to a fire more than anything, but just wasn't sure if he would be able to do what was expected of him. He wanted to prove himself, to do the right thing, to demonstrate that he belonged. It was why he was thoroughly checking the rig. He and every other proby working that day were checking rigs and sweeping floors and cleaning toilets, because it's what they could control. Fires would come or they wouldn't come, but they could begin to prove themselves by constantly doing the routine chores in the firehouse. But still, they hoped to go to a fire. Civilians might not understand, might even think it reckless or irresponsible, a firefighter who wanted to go to a fire. But that was the way it was. A doctor likes to be challenged by a difficult diagnosis; a teacher to get through to a tough student; a lawyer to argue a complex case; a pilot wants to fly, and a firefighter wants to put out fires. John Johnson and every other proby, every other firefighter, didn't wish ill on anyone, didn't hope for tragedy to strike. What they wanted was that *if* a fire occurred, that they just happen to be working. He was still checking the rig at 8:46 AM.

Chris Barry recalls that Daniel Suhr walked into the kitchen rolling up the sleeves of his dark blue FDNY work shirt. The shirt was unbuttoned, and it revealed a green T-shirt beneath. The T-shirt was one purchased as part of a fundraiser for a firefighter from Engine Company 302, Gregg McLoughlin, who died in the line of duty on January 4, 2001. Chris Barry had worked the night before and remembered that while he was on watch, maybe around 10:00 PM, Daniel Suhr entered the firehouse after leaving the retirement party, which was held in a bar across the street. "Danny told me he wanted to get home because his daughter had her first day of pre-school on Tuesday. He wanted to see her in the morning before she went to school and then he'd return to the firehouse for the day tour," Chris said.

Daniel Suhr rolled up his sleeves as he walked into the kitchen, a wide smile spreading across his face; he was large, reassuring. The conversation grew louder as the firefighters caught up with each other, told stories, laughed, a mix of those coming on duty and those getting ready to go home. And then a firefighter called out, "Oh shit. Look at this!" On the TV was an image of smoke pouring out of the upper floors of the World Trade Center. The kitchen grew silent and two or three firefighters said the same thing at the same time, quietly, like a prayer, "My God."

Chapter 5

ASSIGNED

BOTH TV's in the kitchen of the firehouse were tuned to *NY 1*, the local New York City twenty-four-hour news channel. The firefighters agreed that the volume of smoke pouring from the building was ominous; black smoke generated by burning jet fuel.

"Man, the day just started. All the people in there, all the office workers..."

"The brothers are going to get their ass kicked." Firefighting is not just a profession, but a calling, and fellow firefighters aren't just co-workers, but family, brothers and sisters.

"We're either going to go. Or we're going to get relocated," someone said.

The Fire Department transmitted a fifth alarm. That's a lot of companies, twenty engines; ten trucks; rescue companies; numerous chiefs and special units; the Chief of Department. There was a good chance that Engine 216 would be assigned or would get relocated. When a fire occurs in a particular neighborhood, the FDNY ensures that there is still coverage by 'relocating' other companies into the firehouses that are now empty. In large-scale incidents companies from all over the city are sent into the area that would otherwise be stripped of fire protection. I wanted to get the roll call done and make the 0900 entries before we started moving. Then a voice called out through the

27

open kitchen door, "You can see it from up here!"

The firefighters headed up the stairs to the second floor and then up a steep metal stairway, almost a ladder, to the roof. There it was; the top of the north tower burning, black smoke trailing to the south in the perfect blue sky. The view was unobstructed, and the size of the buildings made them appear closer than they were and made the smoke appear to billow in slow motion. A battalion chief standing in the middle of the group said, "You can see the orange of the flames from here. What a horrible fire."

After the plane flew into the north tower, Daniel Suhr told the others that they needed to double check the tools and equipment. He knew that John Johnson had already done it, but he just wanted to be sure. Daniel had responded with Engine 216 to the first attack on the World Trade Center on February 26, 1993. He felt confident that they would respond again. So they made sure the mask cylinders were filled with air, the diesel fuel was topped off, the cooler had fresh ice and water, the first aid equipment was in place, and that the hose lines, nozzles and fittings were ready. While they were checking the rig the regular captain of Engine 216, Ted Jankowski, called the firehouse. John Johnson answered the phone.

Jankowski asked to speak with the most senior firefighter working in Engine 216, Daniel Suhr. "It looks like terrorism, keep the members close," he said, and he warned Daniel to be aware of secondary devices. He knew they would probably be dispatched before he got to the firehouse, so he also said, "Take care of the guys. I'm on my way."

"Don't worry Cap, I'll take care of them," Daniel Suhr answered. Jankowski thanked him and told him to be careful.

In order to be with the members on the rig, Daniel asked Ted Murray if he wanted to drive. Ted had been a chauffeur for about a year and a half, he wanted to be involved with actually extinguishing the fire, he wanted to be on the back step, not out in the street supplying water.

He didn't want to drive. Of course, the job of the Engine Company Chauffeur is vital, as soon as a good supply of water is established, and water is put on the fire, all problems start to disappear. Still, he felt that this was going to be the biggest fire of his career and he wanted to be in on it. Yet Daniel Suhr got on the job ten years prior to Ted, he had ten more years in the Fire Department, ten more years seniority, so when Daniel asked, "What do you want to do?" Ted replied, "What do *you* want to do?"

Daniel answered, "You drive."

The members of Engine 216 were standing in front of the rig when I approached and Daniel offered to help with the assignments, just as he had on the previous day. He explained that he was the regular chauffeur in these groups but that Ted Murray had just got out of chauffeur school, and that Captain Jankowski had a policy where new chauffeurs drive as much as possible their first month or two. He said that Ted drove the night before, and asked if it was okay with me for Ted to drive again? I said, "Okay Danny, we'll let Ted drive."

We then determined the rest of the positions, Chris would take the nozzle, Tony the back-up and Danny would take the control. I wrote each member's name next to the assignment on the BF-4, put the original BF-4 in my pocket and handed Chris Barry the copy. He wrote the names on the large white board on the wall on the far side of the rig then placed the copy of the BF-4 on the dashboard in the cab in front of the officer's seat. I went into the housewatch.

The housewatch is an enclosed area at the front of the apparatus floor that is used as the point of contact between the public and the firehouse. It contains a computer for receiving alarms, a phone, an intercom, a desk, a chair and the 'still alarm,' a button mounted on the wall used to activate the bells or a buzzer, to alert the companies when they have a response. In Engine 216 one buzzer indicated the Engine had a run, two for the Truck, three for the Chief, and four for everybody. A firefighter is always on watch. They receive alarms, turn out the companies, answer the telephone and record all activities that go on in the firehouse in the company journal. I was sitting at the desk, writing the 0900 entries in the company journal when the next cry went up. "The other tower got hit! A plane flew into the south tower!" And there it was on national TV, the image that's burned into America's consciousness. I was shocked by the violence of it. I looked down at the journal and continued writing.

John Johnson, the proby, appeared in the doorway of the house-watch and Mike Donlon, the captain of Ladder 108, stood behind him and nodded as the proby spoke, "I was supposed to be detailed to Engine 204, but Captain Donlon says the chief told him all engine companies are riding with five."

"All right, John. Call 204, let them know you won't be coming," I said. Prior to 1994 all engine companies in the FDNY were staffed with five fighters and an officer. In 1994 the Mayor of New York slashed the budget and caused the staffing on most engine companies to be reduced to four firefighters and an officer. Since that time the city gave the FDNY the discretion to put the fifth firefighter back on the engines for unusual emergencies or natural disasters, such as citywide blackouts or particularly large snowstorms. Two airliners striking two of the tallest buildings in the world met the threshold to ride with five firefighters. I told John Johnson to take the door position, the third firefighter on the hose line. The nozzle position was first, then the back-up, then the door and finally the control. I finished writing in the company journal and walked back towards the front of the rig when the tone alarm sounded, and one buzzer rang out.

"Engine 216, you're going to the fire," the member on watch said as he rushed toward us. He handed me the response ticket, Box 5-5-8087. Tony Sanseviro, Ted Murray, Chris Barry, John Johnson and Daniel

Suhr looked at each other, and they looked at me.

I read the ticket, "They transmitted a Fifth Alarm for Two World Trade Center. It looks like we're assigned ninth or tenth due." I stepped out of my shoes, into my boots and pulled the straps of the bunker pants over my shoulders. I got the familiar twinge of fear and anticipation and excitement in my gut, the tightening of the sphincter, the electric buzz of adrenalin up the spine. I looked back and said, "Bring your shoes guys, we're going to be there awhile."

"We got them Cap," Chris Barry said. He and John Johnson pulled on their bunker gear as they stood next to me. The proby jumped up into the rig on the officer's side and settled into his seat, facing the rear. Chris Barry followed him, pulled down the jump seat and faced front.

Ted Murray stood on the other side of the rig while Daniel Suhr and Tony Sanseviro stood beside him, kicking off their shoes and putting on their bunker gear. Ted looked at Daniel Suhr, "What'd you think, Dan? We'll take the Williamsburg?"

"Yeah. Shoot right down Broadway; it'll be a mess. But there's going to be traffic everywhere. It's the best way into Manhattan," Daniel said.

I pushed my arms through the sleeves of my turnout coat and put my shoes on the floor of the cab beneath the front seat. I was picturing how to get to the Trade Center once we were in Manhattan. I grew up in Stuyvesant Town on the Lower East Side and knew Manhattan well enough to figure it out. But I didn't know Brooklyn. I stepped up into the rig and sat down.

"Ted? Is that right? I'm Paul," I said. Ted was climbing into his seat behind the steering wheel and we shook hands. "Can you get us into Manhattan?"

"Broadway. We'll take Broadway right into the Williamsburg Bridge, Cap," he said. He looked serious and determined.

Ted pressed the start button, and the diesel engine began revving and I looked back at the four firefighters sitting in the rig behind me. Tony Sanseviro sat behind the chauffeur facing the rear and Daniel Suhr sat across from him, facing front. Chris Barry and John Johnson were behind me. A firefighter and a lieutenant walked close to the rig as it was about to pull out and one of them said 'be careful' or 'watch yourself' or something like that. They were clearly anxious; everyone was affected by the graphic images of the burning buildings on TV.

Chapter 6
RESPONSE

WE PULLED out of the firehouse, made a right turn on Union Avenue and a right on Broadway, under the elevated subway. I switched the department radio to the Manhattan frequency and pressed the black headset against my ear, trying to listen, to monitor the transmissions being made about the fire we were responding to. Ted was driving fast and close on the officer's side. The lane of traffic heading towards Manhattan was nearly stopped. The oncoming traffic was light, so we pushed our way into it. The siren was set to 'wail' and I pressed the foot pedal for the air horn, trying to clear a path. We were moving quickly, and we nearly nicked a few cars.

"We're a little close on my side," I said. Ted acknowledged with a nod of his head as the rig bumped and bounced through the potholes in the street. The oncoming cars attempted to get out of our way but the steel pillars on either side of Broadway, the pillars that supported the elevated train tracks, constricted all of us towards the center of the street. A sanitation truck, dented and dirty, was going in the same direction as us, and it hung over the double yellow lines; the side view mirror on the officer's side of our rig smacked the mirror on the driver's side of the sanitation truck. Ted slowed down and I looked at the sanitation worker behind the wheel, but he gestured at us to keep going.

"Sorry about that Cap."

"No harm done. But if we don't get there, we can't do anybody any good. We're going to be fighting traffic all the way Ted, let's take it easy." I knew he would have slowed down even if I didn't say anything, but they were the words that were called for. There was construction in the area, road crews at work, detours, and as we continued towards the Williamsburg Bridge Daniel kept calling out from the back, telling Ted the best route to take.

"*All units responding to Manhattan Box 8087, Two World Trade Center, be advised you are to report in to the Command Post at West and Liberty. Report into Chief Barbara at West Street and Liberty Street. I repeat, all units responding to the Fifth Alarm, Box 8087, report into Chief Barbara at the Command Post at West and Liberty.*" The voice of the dispatcher was clear and calm. He was giving out this information so that the dozens of rigs responding to the south tower would not get involved with the fifth alarm assignment already operating at One World Trade Center, the north tower. They were reaching out to try to impose some order and control over the chaotic conditions at the scene.

Engine Company 216 was bouncing along Broadway, the radio headset still pressed against my ear, trying to block out the sound of the rumbling subway trains overhead and the air horn and siren. We expected gridlock on the bridge, but instead two or three police cars blocked the entrances, they had the bridge closed, and they waved us through onto the Brooklyn bound lanes. We were the only vehicle on the bridge. The Manhattan frequency was busy; the dispatchers were swamped. When they transmitted, I could hear the constant ringing of telephones in the background—civilians calling for help, so I switched back to the Brooklyn frequency for a moment. I wanted to let the Brooklyn dispatcher know that the Williamsburg Bridge was a good route into Manhattan. I attempted to get through a few times, but the Brooklyn frequency was also too busy and we were beginning to descend into Manhattan. I switched back to the Manhattan frequency, to hear updated information, to listen for instructions. I barely glanced at the burning buildings in the distance. I was more concerned with the traffic that lay ahead, at the brake lights of the cars stalled in front of us where the bridge roadway leads into the streets of Lower Manhattan.

Ted was in a tough spot. He was driving his company to a very serious fire, outside of his usual response area, not even in his assigned borough, with an officer in charge who he had met just minutes ago. We made a left on Allen Street at the base of the bridge, then a right on Canal. We wanted to approach from the south of the World Trade Center so we wouldn't get backed up behind the units responding from the north, we wanted to get to the tip of Manhattan then head back uptown. We continued south and east, Bowery, St James Place, Pearl Street, Water Street, the siren droning, the air horn blasting, trying to loosen the pack of cars and trucks in the streets ahead of us. The buildings on either side of the street got taller the further downtown we went.

Pedestrians watched as the rig crawled through the traffic, the lights and siren nearly useless. Groups of people gathered on corners looking at the smoke in the sky, then turned and watched gravely as Engine 216 passed. Chris Barry recalls that he and John Johnson, sitting on the right side of the rig that was heading south, had a good view of the twin towers, that every intersection created a corridor through which they could see the burning buildings. He said that because the day was so clear everything was especially intense, the sky hyper blue; the twin towers silver white; the smoke dark black. A friend of his, a firefighter in Ladder Company 146, jogged up to the rig. He was working a side job in the area; he called to Chris, asked him what was going on. Chris told him that he needed to get back to his firehouse.

Tony Sanseviro said, "Danny was talking to me, telling me this was going to be a really bad fire." Tony was a little anxious to hear him talking like that. He never remembered Daniel being concerned about a fire before, then again, there had never been a fire like this before. John Johnson strained to listen, but the diesel engine was located in the center of the rig separating the firefighters, so it was difficult for him to hear what Daniel was saying. At some point he asked Chris, "How are we going to put this out?" and Chris just shook his head. Engine 216 went slower and slower and finally came to a dead stop. The Staten Island Ferry Terminal was within view, just to the south of us. There was complete gridlock. I leaned on the air horn for a few seconds, but nothing was moving. I turned to Ted and told him I was going to get out and see if there was anything we could do to get us through the stopped traffic.

"I'll go this way," Daniel called from the back. He got out of the rig on his side and I got out on mine. He walked left, towards the Ferry Terminal. He was telling drivers to move, to back up, to stop, to go. He was directing traffic, trying to clear a path for his company. I looked down a narrow block and saw traffic moving up and to the left, toward our rig. We would have to stop additional cars from turning down the one-way street, clear the cars that were already there, then go the one block against traffic and try to get moving again. The streets were tight: Whitehall Street; State Street; Bridge; Stone. Two Traffic Agents appeared and we explained the problem and we went to work and in a short time had cleared the street. I radioed Ted on the handie-talkie and he drove slowly, inching through the narrow street. The rig stopped and Daniel and I got back on.

"We'll make a right when the street's clear, then a left. Hopefully we'll get through from there," I said. Ted navigated through the streets, squeezing the fire engine through the small spaces, through some of the oldest streets in the city, streets that were originally footpaths, carved out hundreds of years ago. Footpaths that were eventually packed with mud and shells then paved with cobblestones, created for horses and wagons, not 50,000-pound twenty-first century fire engines. But he made it look easy.

Then suddenly we were free of the cars and pedestrians and tight streets. We were racing north on West Street, past the entrance to the Brooklyn-Battery Tunnel and towards the location of the Command Post. Rigs were lined up along a concrete divider that ran down the middle of West Street on our left. The street ahead was congested with fire apparatus, engines and trucks, and ambulances, and police cars—all of them with their lights flashing.

"Ted, stop here," I said. We stopped in the middle of the street, two or three blocks from the south tower. There was a space next to us that was just big enough for our rig between two other fire engines. The firefighters got off the rig and began to take the folded lengths of 2 ½ inch hose from the side of the rig, standard operating procedure in the FDNY for a fire in a high-rise building. It was dim, almost dark. I imagined that the height of the buildings always created some shade in the area, but the smoke was making it darker still. I faced the firefighters as I spoke, "Ted's going to tuck the rig in here, let's give him a hand, then we'll get going."

Chris Barry and Tony Sanseviro acted as guides on either side while Daniel Suhr planted himself in the rear, waving him in. John Johnson tightened the waist strap of his mask and looked up at the burning buildings. "Make sure you have a light and an extra cylinder," I said. But they had it already, flashlights and spare air cylinders and fifty-foot lengths of hose. Danny carried the standpipe kit instead of the hose. The standpipe kit had the necessary tools and fittings to connect a hose once inside the building.

We started walking north. My mind was searching for the problems that might confront us. I felt the standpipes would be out of service and thought about an alternate source of water. Could we lower lengths of hose down from the upper floors? It would take a lot of coordination, a lot of time. Ted Murray stayed with the rig; he would need to find a hydrant, stretch hose lines and augment other engine companies closer to the building. It would take many engine company chauffeurs; it would take whole engine companies and chief officers committed solely to the effort to somehow supply water to the upper floors. A truck company went racing past heading toward the building; it may have been Ladder 105. I knew we'd be climbing a lot of stairs and thought for a moment that we might have tried to park closer, to save a few steps.

Smoke poured from the upper floors and flaming debris fell downward as if in slow motion. Cars were burning and an engine company was extinguishing a large rubbish fire. It was hard to tell which Company it was and what was burning, but they were operating just north of the south pedestrian bridge that arched over West Street. Chris Barry remembered NYPD officers warning us not to step on something in the street; it may have been a body.

Several rubbish fires burned throughout the area, cars or plane parts or pieces of the building, and smoke hung in the air. It was irritating to the nose and throat. There was a constant sound of sirens and air horns getting closer. The flashing lights from the emergency vehicles on the surrounding streets only exaggerated the fact that the visibility was poor due to the smoke in the air. The whole scene was gray and desolate.

We walked up and found the chief in charge of the Command Post. He had set up on West Street just north of Albany Street. He had set up in an optimal place for a Command Post, in front of One Financial Center. It was set back from the street, a grassy area separating it from West Street, partially protected, with some decorative concrete walls that created a place to stage units. It was a good location. Liberty Street was north of the pedestrian bridge but the chief was south of the bridge, closer to Albany Street, across from Cedar Street.

Two engine companies were just behind the chief, Engine 205 and Engine 217. Some of the firefighters from the companies leaned against the low retaining walls, and others stood. They had unbuckled their turnout coats, trying to stay cool, and their hose and spare cylinders lay on the ground at their feet. They were waiting for an assignment. At large scale operations it is not unusual for companies to be held in reserve, at a staging area or exterior Command Post. If too many units went straight into the building it could become difficult to keep track of them, to control them, to utilize them most effectively. Inside the building a Lobby Command Post is established, and when the chief in charge of the Lobby Command Post decides that they need more companies, they call for them. Engine 205 and Engine 217 were eager to get into Two World Trade Center, to go to work, but they weren't needed yet so they had to wait for orders. I approached the chief and reported in. "Engine 216, we're tenth due on the Fifth Alarm."

"Okay Cap. Tell your company to stand fast. Put down your gear, open your coats, it may be a while," the chief said. His name, Barbara, was stenciled on the back of his turnout coat. He was Gerard Barbara, the Chief of Fire Prevention, and his white helmet was surprisingly blackened for a staff chief. There were about a dozen staff chiefs in the department, they ran large bureaus, such as Training, Personnel, Fire Prevention, and Safety, and they served as City-Wide Tour Commanders.

Chief Barbara was responsible for fire prevention in a city of over eight million people, responsible for the thousands of buildings, for every structure, to ensure they complied with the complex fire codes and laws governing New York. When a third alarm was transmitted, City-Wide Tour Commanders were the chief-in-charge of the fire until it was under control or until it became a larger incident. If it escalated to a fourth alarm, the Chief of Operations took over, and the Chief of Department responded once it reached a fifth alarm or above. The Chief of Department was running the entire FDNY response to the fires in the twin towers; staff chiefs were in charge of sectors, smaller pieces of the operation. Chief Barbara had the Command Post outside of the south tower, and Chief Donald Burns was in charge of the Lobby Command Post inside the building.

I began to turn around, to tell Engine 216 to stand fast, but Chief Barbara must have received a message over his radio, on the command channel, the frequency that the chiefs were using to communicate with each other. He said, "No. Wait. You're going in. Report into the Lobby Command Post." He pointed toward the entrance to Two World Trade Center, diagonally across West Street, maybe 200 yards away.

"All right guys, let's go," I said. Tony, Chris and John had the hose over their shoulders and the spare cylinders in hand. Daniel Suhr carried the spare cylinder and the standpipe kit. The members of Engine 205 and Engine 217 began buckling their coats and picking up their equipment.

Chris Barry heard Daniel say, "We're all going to stay together... We're probably going to get burned...This has the makings of the worst day of our lives." Daniel Suhr stepped off toward the building. He stepped off fast and said, "This is a terrible day. Let's do this fast."

Chapter 7

BELLE HARBOR

DANIEL AND Nancy married on April 2, 1989. The wedding took place in St. Edmunds Roman Catholic Church on Ocean Avenue in Brooklyn. They had been going out on and off since meeting in elementary school eleven years earlier. By the time they got married Danny had been a firefighter for over three years and Nancy was working for a title search firm in lower Manhattan. Daniel's mother Sheila had recommended her for the job.

Once married, they moved into an apartment in the Belle Harbor section of the Rockaways. Nancy loved their first apartment, their first home. She said that if you stood at just the right angle you could even catch a glimpse of Jamaica Bay from one of the windows; a water view. Daniel was always busy. He eventually became the Union Delegate of Engine Company 216, which necessitated extra hours at Union meetings and delegate seminars. He played football for the Brooklyn Mariners and the FDNY team, The Bravest, and also worked as a bartender on Friday nights at the Avenue U Bar in Brooklyn. "I never went into the bar when Danny was working," remembers Nancy, recalling the tacit agreement they shared. "He considered the bar to be his place," she said. "And I didn't want to go there anyway." But sometimes, on her way home from Manhattan, she would let herself into his car parked out on the street and leave a little note, "I'll see you soon" or "Be careful driving home" or just simply, "I love you."

Nancy and Daniel grew up in working class homes, good homes, but Daniel wanted them to have more. He had several business ideas including opening a bar or a bagel store. After looking into it, he and Nancy decided that the bar business had too many headaches, and the hours seemed too disruptive for the family life that they wanted. The bagel store also had downsides, including the early morning hours it required. Daniel next considered a pizza shop, and towards that end he got another side job working in a pizza shop that was owned by the father of a good friend. He worked there for over three years and learned the business.

In 1993 Nancy and Daniel bought a pizza shop on the corner of Avenue U and East 29 Street. They named it N&D Pizza. It had been around for years but was no longer doing well. Daniel felt like they could make it work, and Nancy believed in him. Nancy said that he had that effect on people, that he made people around him believe. Instead of a conventional bank loan, they borrowed from family, and friends, and friends of friends. Two men from Albania had worked there for several years, making pizza, and Nancy and Danny kept them on. Chris Suhr became their eyes and ears in the shop, working 75 hours a week, doing whatever was needed. Daniel and Nancy both worked there, but Daniel had the firehouse and Nancy had her full-time job, so Chris was a huge help. Chris described those years simply, "Dan was the boss, I was the horse." Daniel's brother James also worked there, he was in college, and he worked at N&D whenever he could.

Within the first year N&D had turned a profit. They started to pay off their loans as quickly as they could; those who charged interest were paid first. The pizza shop was a lot of work, they put in more hours than they had anticipated, but it was worth the effort. They created a nice neighborhood restaurant that served good food for a fair price; they were making money and improving their lives.

As time went on they decided that they would like to have a child. Nancy recalls the difficulties; there was surgery, drugs, and numerous attempts. They had made a choice to have a child, but began to wonder if it would ever happen. One year went by, then two, and then three. They weren't so sure anymore, but they kept trying and finally, after four years, on November 17, 1998, Briana was born.

With the birth of their daughter, their focus shifted. They needed more room so they moved to a house, still in Belle Harbor. Nancy stopped working at the title search firm and cut her hours at N&D. And although Daniel still worked at the pizza shop, and the firehouse, and still played football and worked as the Union Delegate, Nancy and Briana always came first.

There were a lot of senior firefighters in Engine 216 and Ladder 108 that Danny looked up to, that he learned from. One member that he especially admired was Harry Ford. Harry got on the job on January 27, 1974; he was also on the Bravest football team and was an exceptional firefighter. He was a role model for Daniel both in and out of the firehouse. In 1990 he transferred to Rescue Company 4 in Queens. There are only five rescue companies in the city, one in each borough. They are staffed with experienced and knowledgeable firefighters, and are responsible for specialized, highly technical operations; high angle rescue; confined space; building collapse, scuba operations. One of the most important functions they perform, the original purpose for which they were created, is to rescue fellow firefighters when they get in trouble.

On June 17, 2001, Father's Day, a little after 4:00 PM, a fire broke out in a hardware store in Astoria, Queens. Rescue Company 4 responded and after they arrived a massive explosion occurred. Numerous firefighters were seriously injured, some so badly that they would never be able to return to work. More tragic still, three firefighters perished; Firefighter John Downing from Ladder Company 163, promoted posthumously to Lieutenant, and Firefighters Brian Fahey and Harry Ford from Rescue Company 4. The fire would come to be known as The Father's Day Fire.

Daniel Suhr was working that Father's Day in Engine 216. He was working when the signal 5-5-5-5 was transmitted. The signal 5-5-5-5 is transmitted in every firehouse in the city to let all members know that a firefighter has died in the line of duty. When Daniel learned that Harry Ford had died, he broke down and cried. John Johnson was also working that day and he remembers Daniel standing in the middle of the kitchen, crying. This big, tough, senior man was openly weeping at the loss of his friend and mentor Harry Ford. Nancy recalls that when Daniel called to tell her that Harry had died, he was so broken up that he could barely get the words out. They attended the wake together. When Daniel lined up outside of the church for Harry's funeral, and for those of Brian Fahey and John Downing, he did so with thousands and thousands of other firefighters.

Daniel went on vacation in late August of 2001. Nancy said, "We had a couple of good weeks. We spent a lot of time at the beach and Danny and I laughed at the silly things Briana was doing." Briana was talkative, always had something to say, and Nancy and Daniel got a kick out of her constant commentary. Daniel returned to work on Monday September 10. He told Nancy that one of the guys in the firehouse, Bruce Foss, was retiring, and that there was a party for him in a local bar. Daniel said he would go to the party for a little while, but then he wanted to get home because Briana had her first day of preschool the next day, and Daniel wanted to see her in the morning.

On Tuesday morning Daniel was getting ready to leave for work. Briana sat up in bed, just opening her eyes, and she looked sleepy and innocent and her hair was wild. Nancy remembers how Danny smiled, not just the Daniel Suhr smile that so many knew so well, but the smile that he saved for Nancy and Briana. Nancy had taken Briana to get a haircut the day before and Danny looked at Briana and said, "Nice bangs..." And he said the word bangs like a song, happy, pleased, maybe teasing a little. His daughter was growing up, going to school, would turn three in a couple of months, and his wife was taking care of her, preparing her for a new phase in her young life. He was proud, grateful, at peace.

Daniel left for the firehouse in Williamsburg and Nancy gave Briana breakfast. In a little while Nancy got Briana dressed and out of the house. They headed out to the stores, to do some shopping, to buy food for dinner, and to get home in time to bring Briana to the afternoon session of pre-school. At the butcher shop there was a small TV at the end of the counter. As the man behind the counter took Nancy's order, she looked at the TV and saw the news. They were reporting that a plane had just flown into the north tower of the World Trade Center in lower Manhattan.

Chapter 8

NO GREATER LOVE

I **DIDN'T** know that Daniel Suhr was a football player, a middle linebacker. I didn't know his nickname was Captain America. I didn't know how quick he was, how focused. When Chief Gerard Barbara ordered us into Two World Trade Center, Daniel stepped off toward the building and said, "This is a terrible day. Let's do this fast." He carried over seventy pounds of equipment. He wore a mask and bunker gear and helmet, carried the spare cylinder and standpipe kit, yet he moved quickly, looking forward, then looking up. He wanted to get in the lobby, run up the stairs, stretch a line, put water on the fire, find victims, get them out. He wanted to do whatever we were ordered to do, whatever we could possibly do to help somebody.

We didn't know what was about to happen; no one knew that these were the last moments of Daniel's life—a life well lived, a good life. He was both the cause of the good and the result of it. His parents; his brothers and sisters; his friends; his teachers; football; the coaches and players, practice and games, playing hard, to the last second on the clock; the FDNY, the fires and the training, the officers and firefighters, and most of all, there was his wife, Nancy, her profound influence on him, their two-year-old daughter; all of it leading to the life he lived. This moment was how he always lived; he embraced life, fully, completely, head on, doing it right.

We were all walking rapidly toward the entrance to Two World Trade Center—toward the Lobby Command Post. Tony and Chris and John were each carrying a spare cylinder in one hand and the fifty-foot length of hose on their shoulder. The members of Engine 205 and Engine 217 had to buckle their turnout coats; they had to lean over and pick up their hose and air cylinders. Engine 217 also brought forcible entry tools and first aid equipment. We walked diagonally toward the entrance, through a grassy area in front of One Financial Center and across the southbound lanes on West Street.

There was a concrete divider down the middle of West Street separating the southbound lanes from the northbound lanes. It was the same divider that we parked next to when we had arrived. The divider might have been fifteen feet wide and of varying height, maybe two feet high where we were. There was soil and grass, bushes and small trees inside of it, and decorative black chains on decorative black posts. There were periodic openings in the divider, corresponding to the streets that ran east and west, perpendicular to West Street. The closest opening was maybe a hundred yards south, at Albany Street. To get to the opening we would need to backtrack to the right, but we continued to go straight ahead.

We stepped up on the divider and walked through it, on the soil and the grass, then down on to the northbound side of the street. We headed east on Cedar Street, looking up to make sure nothing was coming down, then looking forward to avoid tripping on anything in the street: plane parts; building parts; burning material. Smoke filled the air and sirens wailed; it was dim and dark. The streets were deserted except for firefighters and cops and EMTs. The term surreal might come to mind—surreal and dangerous.

Engine 216 led the way. Engine 205 and Engine 217 had retrieved their gear and now followed close behind. We were 16 firefighters heading toward the lobby of the south tower. We were in a sort of a line, spread out, but moving together, looking forward and looking up. We began winding our way through cars. It occurred to me that it was a parking lot, but it was nearly empty. The parking lot was in front of St. Nicholas Greek Orthodox Church on Cedar Street, the only church in lower Manhattan that would be destroyed that day.

Daniel Suhr was to my right. We walked in step, shoulder to shoulder, moving fast. Tony, Chris and John were just behind us, and then Engine 217 and Engine 205. We were within a hundred yards of the doors leading into Two World Trade Center. Then there was a loud bang, like an explosion. And Daniel went down.

"Oh shit."

"Oh fuck."

"Oh God, Danny."

Danny lay on the ground. A jumper had struck him—a poor soul who was so desperate to escape the flames and the heat that he stepped out of a window hundreds of feet high. Danny's helmet lay nearby. "I heard a whistling sound, something falling toward us. And then I saw Danny fall," Chris remembers. John recalls a wheel or tire rolling rapidly away from us and Tony remembers the jumper striking a car. I heard the impact, was walking next to Danny when it happened, but knew that Tony, Chris and John had seen it, and knew it was heartbreaking to witness. The firefighters dropped the hose and spare air cylinders. I dropped the cylinder but held onto the flashlight and Sunilla tool. Danny was unconscious. Tony got down on one knee in the street next to him and pressed two fingers against Danny's neck, feeling for the carotid artery. Tony looked up and I saw the hope in his eyes as he knelt next to his friend, "He's got a pulse, Cap," he said.

The building across the street, 90 West Street, was undergoing renovation. It was on the southeast corner of West and Cedar, one block south of Liberty. There was scaffolding erected on the west side of the building, facing West Street, and on the north side of the building, facing Two World Trade Center. Black mesh was installed on the exterior of the scaffolding, to stop construction material from landing on the surrounding streets. In addition, a sidewalk shed ran along the west and north perimeter, beneath the scaffolding. The sidewalk shed was a solid structure, required by law, providing protection from falling debris to persons using the sidewalk below.

"Let's get him under the scaffolding," I said. Chris Barry said the same thing at the same time; we were maybe fifty yards away from it. It would afford some protection while we worked on Danny. Chris, Tony and John picked Danny up and I depressed the button on the microphone of the handie-talkie hanging over my shoulder. I tried to control my voice as I spoke, "Mayday, Mayday, Mayday. Engine Two-Sixteen to Command Post with a Mayday."

Tony, Chris and John were crossing the parking lot, flaming debris and metal coming down around them. They carried Danny away from Two World Trade Center, toward 90 West Street. I walked alongside them, looking for obstacles, trying to listen for Chief Barbara's acknowledgement over the radio. Danny was a large man and the firefighters from Engine 205 and Engine 217 caught up with us and helped carry him. They took off his mask as they moved him.

Chief Barbara answered, "Unit with the Mayday, come in."

"Engine Two-Sixteen with a Mayday. We have a Firefighter with a life-threatening injury. We need an ambulance. We're across from Two World Trade Center. The ambulance can respond to West and Liberty."

"Ten-Four," he said.

The firefighters worked fast, they removed his coat and laid him gently on the sidewalk beneath the scaffolding. Two firefighters ran toward us from West Street, one of them carried a long board, the bright orange device used to transport injured persons. They may have been from Engine 217. The firefighters placed Danny on the long board, strapped him to it and Tony and Chris began CPR.

An ambulance pulled up at the far corner of the building. The paramedics trotted toward us wheeling a stretcher, bouncing it along the uneven sidewalk beneath the scaffolding. The firefighters lifted the long board with Danny laying on it and placed it on the stretcher. We raced toward the ambulance, the medics pushing the stretcher, with Chris and Tony jogging alongside, giving chest compressions. It was dark beneath the scaffolding, dark beneath the smoke. We couldn't really see the south tower, but we could feel it, burning and crumbling.

We reached the ambulance, a medic opened one door and a firefighter opened the other. I looked up and down West Street and saw a lot of rigs, their lights flashing, a haze in the air. I was worried that the ambulance would have trouble getting through all the other emergency vehicles that were still responding in, trouble getting away from the burning buildings, getting to the hospital.

"Engine Two-Sixteen to Command Post," I said.

"Command Post to Two-Sixteen."

"Engine Two-Sixteen, we need a police escort for the ambulance. We're at West and Liberty." Although we were actually at the inter-section of West and Cedar.

Chief Barbara answered, "Command Post, 10-4." It would be the last transmission that I would hear him make.

Doctor Kerry Kelly, the Chief Medical Officer of the FDNY, climbed into the ambulance along with Tony and Chris. A paramedic was also in the ambulance and two EMT's, Richard Erdy and his partner Soraya Solano. Dr. Kelly and the paramedic tried to establish an airway. After some time they stopped and Dr. Kelly told the EMTs to transport Danny to the hospital. I spotted an NYPD Highway car racing north on West Street. I flagged it down and explained that we had a mortally injured firefighter and needed help getting to the hospital. The highway cop asked, "Where are they going?" I walked back to the ambulance and called inside and told them they would have a police escort.

"What hospital are you taking him to?"

"St. Vinnie's," they said. I let the Highway cop know. It wasn't until years later that I learned that they transported Danny to Bellevue Hospital.

Doctor Kelly exited the ambulance and let me know with the slightest shake of her head that Danny had either already expired or that he wasn't going to make it. It struck me that now this was a fatal fire, the dreaded parlance used in the fire department when a firefighter dies while fighting a fire. Yet some part of me wanted to believe that he still might make it. Dr Kelly wore shoes that had low heels that would make it easy to trip on the crosshatched diamond plate of the bumper and I reached out and offered my arm for support. She held my arm as she stepped on to the bumper then down to the street.

I tried to physically push John Johnson inside the ambulance with the others. I wanted him off West Street, away from the scene. I felt like it was the best I could do to protect him. Officers are responsible for the firefighters working with them, especially the probies. One of my men was already gravely injured; I was desperate to get John out of the area. I said something like "Here's another pair of hands." But someone from inside said, "It's too crowded already. There's no room."

EMT Soraya Solano got out and I pointed to the highway patrol car that was waiting about fifty feet north of us. She motioned to the highway cop and the cop acknowledged. She climbed into the driver's seat of the ambulance and slammed the door shut. Tony and Chris were in the ambulance working on Danny and John Johnson closed the rear doors and the ambulance pulled away and headed north.

I looked over to where Danny had been struck, where we had dropped our gear; flaming material lay in the street alongside the hose and air cylinders. It didn't make sense to report into the lobby command post, an officer and a proby, there wasn't much we could do. I wanted to find the chauffeur, make sure he was all right. I thought we might go to the hospital and check on Danny, check on Chris and Tony. I really wasn't sure what we were going to do, I was shaken, maybe in shock.

John Johnson carried the air masks that Tony Sanseviro and Chris Barry had dropped when they were caring for Danny. He carried both masks and was wearing his own. I had picked up Danny's turnout coat and carried it in my left hand and held the flashlight and Senilla tool in the other. I looked at John Johnson and said, "Let's go back to the rig, find Ted, regroup." We turned and began to walk south, away from the building. We took two or three steps when the rumbling began.

Chapter 9

THE SOUTH TOWER

JOHN AND I started to run. The rumbling was a physical presence behind us, louder and louder. He dropped the two extra masks he was carrying, they landed hard in the street, then he pulled off his own mask. I was carrying Danny's turnout coat. I wanted to bring it back, to save it, it was important. But after a few steps it felt too heavy, I couldn't sprint and carry it at the same time.

The crashing and roaring were growing more intense. John was to my left; he was younger and taller and faster and within moments he was ahead of me. *Thank God.* The sound was gaining on us, we could feel it, the air pressure pushed us forward, the noise pushed us forward. *Hail Mary, full of grace, the Lord is with Thee, blessed art Thou among women, and blessed is the fruit of thy womb Jesus...* I'm not sure if I said it out loud or only in my head. I didn't know exactly what was happening, what was collapsing, but knew without the slightest shred of doubt that we weren't going to outrun it. We were either going to get hit with something big and heavy, or not. But still, we kept running as fast as we could, and the proby was opening up the distance between us, veering to the left.

Hail Mary, full of grace, the Lord is with Thee, blessed art Thou among women, and blessed is the fruit of thy womb Jesus... I repeated the beginning over and over. I couldn't concentrate enough to finish the prayer. I couldn't remember it, didn't have the mental capacity, couldn't remember anything, my name, my wife, my kids, anything— just fear, panic, arms pumping, high stepping, sucking wind. A cloud of dust began to overtake us. We kept running.

I saw a ladder company, a tower ladder, in the middle of West Street. It may have been Ladder Company 15. It was an odd place to leave a rig. For the slightest instant I thought about diving under it, but it didn't feel right. I didn't want to stop. I didn't want to be trapped. John was 20 or 30 feet ahead of me, 20 feet to my left. The path he was on took him to the left of the truck company. I wanted to follow him, to try to keep him in sight. But the number of extra steps to get behind him, to pass the rig on the left, seemed insurmountable, felt like it would take too long. I didn't think I could catch him anyway. So I continued straight and passed to the right of the ladder company.

The dust was getting progressively thicker, the visibility worse and worse, and when I got to the end of the truck the air was black. I was gagging, trying to take short breaths, the mask cylinder banging against my back, my feet sliding in the boots, slamming heel to toe. I felt like the pounding and crashing sound was still happening, that it was everywhere, but it also may have stopped, I wasn't sure. I looked for the proby, I looked ahead and to the left, but I couldn't see him. I couldn't see anything.

I slowed down, then started walking fast, walking slower, then stopped and leaned over in the dark, hands on my knees, coughing, trying to breathe. I turned on the air cylinder and was going to try to take a few breaths, but the face piece was packed with dust. And the air was filled with dust, but it seemed like the rumbling had stopped.

"Johnson. John Johnson. Two-Sixteen," I called out. I coughed, almost puked, turned on my light, but it was useless. I called out again and got no reply. I decided to try to find our rig and the chauffeur, Ted Murray, and then we'd both look for the proby. I moved forward through the dark, slowly, searching. I began to hear voices. I saw an engine company apparatus rise up out of the dust, like a ship out of the fog, sudden and large. I used the light to read the numbers on the side. It wasn't my rig, but then I saw another rig behind it and then another. I finally found Engine 216; Ted and I were face to face.

"Ted, are you all right?"

"Yeah Cap, but holy shit, I thought you were gone." Many years later Ted would describe how he saw the south tower when it started to collapse. He saw the windows blowing out on the upper third of the building and he saw the top of the building start to pancake downward onto itself. Then his view was blocked, he couldn't see the lower half of the building, and the dust started to blow. He got in the driver's seat and a civilian appeared and tried to climb on his lap. Ted walked him around the front of the rig and put him in the officer's seat. Two members of the NYPD approached, a lieutenant and a police officer. They jumped in the back. Someone in the rig told Ted to drive away, to get out of there, and Ted said they weren't going anywhere. He knew this was where Danny and the rest of 216 would try to meet, if they could.

Ted said, "The dust was getting worse and the noise was getting louder. I thought we might get hit by a part of the building, by steel. It was black and loud. Someone was yelling to drive away until one of the cops told him to shut up. Then the noise finally stopped." Ted remembered that the dust slowly began to settle, and when it settled enough to begin to see the lights of the rigs in front of them, the civilian and the two cops opened the doors and jumped out.

I asked Ted, "Have you seen the proby?"

"No." His face was white and his eyes half closed with the dust. "But where's everybody else?"

I forgot that he didn't know what happened. He didn't know about Danny. "Listen Ted, Danny's been hurt. He's been taken to the hospital. The other guys went with him."

"How bad?"

"Pretty bad, maybe real bad. We'll see," I said. Ted was swinging a mask onto his back, pulling on gloves, buckling his coat. We turned and started to head back towards the towers, looking for John. We called his name while we walked. The visibility was beginning to improve and civilians were coming into view. We told them to head south. We were moving fast, retracing my steps; I wasn't sure if the ambulance made it, if anything happened to the proby...

We got to the front of Ladder 15, the last place I saw him. Large steel columns and box beams lay twisted and interlocked all over the street. I climbed over the steel to the far side of the rig, where Johnson had run, and shined the light beneath the beams. Ted made his way alongside the rig, looking and calling John's name. I went into the lobby of the nearest building just beyond the Truck. "Anybody see a firefighter in here?"

"No," a man said. He stood with a small group of civilians. He looked like he wanted me to stay with him. "What happened? What should we do?"

They must have been inside the lobby during the collapse because they weren't covered in dust. They were scared but they were okay, they didn't need me to escort them out of the building. I looked at the man, at the whole group, and said, "Get out of here, head downtown." And I went back outside. We went past the buildings on Albany Street, then continued down West Street, walked another block and looked up and down Carlisle, then to Rector and then the entrance to the Brooklyn-Battery Tunnel. People were asking for guidance along the way, "Is it safe?" *No, the fucking world is ending.* But we just kept saying, "Head south."

We got back to the rig and a civilian appeared. The civilian was covered in white and gagging. He called out, "Help, help me. You got some water or something? I can't breathe, I can't see."

Ted opened the EMS compartment and got out a liter of sterile water. A woman came staggering towards us, followed by another man, a large man in a suit. They were survivors, in shock, in need of help.

"Where should I go?" the woman asked.

I looked at the woman and pointed downtown, "Head south, go to the ferry, don't hang around here." Ted flushed the first man's eyes with sterile water and ripped open a package with a sterile four by four bandage and used it to wipe the mud from around the man's eyes and nose. He used more water. The man blinked and coughed and mumbled a quick thank you as he walked away. White papers were blowing down the sidewalk, through the streets, and the dust was settling everywhere. It was settling on the fire engines and fire trucks parked along the concrete divider on West Street, on the decorative black posts and the decorative black chains inside the divider, on the mailboxes and streetlamps and hydrants, on the planters in front of the buildings, and especially on the firefighters who rushed past, heading north. The visibility was barely a block. Ted coughed forcefully to try to clear his lungs and I began to walk back again; toward the spot I'd last seen Johnson. There was nothing else I could do.

Ted cleaned out the eyes of the man in the suit. More people were approaching, and he kept helping them until after some period of time John Johnson appeared. John started helping Ted with the civilians and Ted saw an off-duty firefighter from Engine 216 rushing past. Ted called, "Hey Mooch." Rob Muccio stopped and came over to the rig. He was wearing a blue T-shirt, shorts and a pair of old rubber fire boots, folded down in half. John was helping the civilians and Ted told Rob that we'd all go to the collapse site together to see what we could do as soon as I got back. When I got back to the rig Ted was helping a police officer wash out his eyes. When he was done he held up the last of the sterile water and a sterile gauze pad. "Let me rinse out your eyes, Cap?"

Years later John Johnson remembers the collapse starting and looking back just once. He dropped the two masks he was carrying and pulled his own mask off his back and threw it to the ground as he ran. He doesn't remember seeing a rig on West Street. "I heard the steel landing around me, I thought I was going to die," he recalled.

> *I thought of my mother, and how I wished I could tell her I loved her. I wanted her to know that. I thought of my father too, a retired cop, 23 years on the NYPD. How proud he was that I had just started a career in the FDNY. My mother was also very proud, but worried about the dangers that came along with the profession. And I thought of how heartbroken she would be.*

John kept running. Fast. He flew. He was almost keeping ahead of the dust, but not quite.

He looked back at one point and saw the dust rising behind him. And then it caught him and he pulled up the hood that was around his neck and breathed through it. Firefighters wear a protective hood around their neck, ready to pull up on their head to fit beneath their helmet when they fight a fire, for thermal protection. Now he tried to use it as a filter as the dust got thicker and he kept moving. But he couldn't see very well so he wasn't running full speed anymore, he was jogging, then walking. He jogged and walked, jogged and walked, until he reached Battery Park and then he stopped. He waited for a moment and tried to catch his breath. In the Fire Academy he was trained to feel for heat in a smoke condition, remove a glove, put your hand over your head; so he checked for heat in the dust and didn't feel any. He began to walk back toward the rig.

Civilians asked him for guidance. He didn't want to tell them that he was brand new; he had no idea what they should do. He didn't really know what *he* should do. But he told them to leave the area, just get out of there. He walked through the dust, people rushing past him away from the collapse. He kept moving and finally saw Engine Company 216.

When I saw John at the rig I shook my head slowly and said, almost to myself, "Thank God you're safe."

He said, "I just kept running."

"Thank God you're safe," I repeated. It was like some crazy vision, a resurrection, a religious experience. I felt an incredible weight lift off my chest. I had been fighting against acknowledging the increasingly likely fact that John Johnson was trapped somewhere, crushed beneath structural steel. I can't describe how relieved I was to see him. The feeling of elation lasted several long seconds and then I was brought back to reality. He survived, thank God, but how many others didn't?

"I hope the ambulance made it," Johnson said. We looked, but the dust caused the view to be obscured; it was just grayness and smoke. And there were white papers, letters; bills; affidavits; orders; lists; invoices; skirting along the ground.

I had lost a glove somewhere and opened the crew door of the rig to look for one. As I was looking Ted said, "Hey Cap, this is a firefighter from Two-Sixteen. He's going with us too." I turned and saw only Ted and John Johnson standing there. Ted looked around and his friend was gone, a block away, heading north. Ted called out, "Mooch! Hey! What are you doing? Stop."

"I got to go, my uncle's in there," Rob Muccio said as he walked away. He was moving fast, almost jogging, heading towards the collapse. Ted began to walk after him and an NYPD cop was rushing past us, heading south.

"The north tower's going to collapse. I just got it over my radio," the cop said as he went by.

"Mooch! Wait! The north tower's going to go," Ted yelled. John was with Ted and they were moving fast and I went after them.

"Ted, stop, we'll all go together," I said. I didn't want to lose anyone else. I was midway between them and our rig; they were about a block or two from the Ladder Company in the middle of West Street.

Ted called out again, "Mooch, stop, the north tower's going to collapse." He remembers seeing civilians on the sidewalk along West Street. When they heard him say the tower was about to collapse, they started to run. He called out a third time and Mooch finally stopped. As he turned Ted saw the top of the north tower begin to lean, begin to come down. Then it started again: the rumbling, thundering, crashing; like a tidal wave, a freight train.

Chapter 10
THE NORTH TOWER

WE COULDN'T see it happening. The air was too thick with dust. Ted ran toward me and we turned and began to run south. I saw John running, he was in front of us, then the dust turned everything black. The blackness and the vicious noise were disorienting and it wasn't clear which way to run, which way was safe. So we slowed and walked side by side. It became difficult to breathe. I scraped the dust out of the face piece of my air mask and opened the purge valve all the way. Air blew out of the face piece full blast and after a few seconds I shut off the purge and gave it to Ted. He took a few deep breaths then handed the mask back to me.

John Johnson would later describe that when the north tower began to collapse he ducked into a building on West Street. He brought a small group of civilians with him, shepherding them through the doors and out of the dust. A building maintenance man told him that some people were stuck in an elevator at the lobby level. The man handed John a crowbar and John tried to pry open the elevator car doors. The doors barely budged. The situation called for an FDNY truck company with five knowledgeable firefighters and a full complement of tools; elevator keys, a couple of hooks and halligans. Two firefighters might go to the floor above to disengage the interlock, they might shut off the power, an officer would coordinate the effort. But all John had was a crowbar. He worked for a few minutes then understood he was wasting his time. He knew the civilians in the elevator weren't in any imminent danger; he had to get back outside; people needed help. He wanted to find us.

When he stepped out of the building to look for Engine 216, another engine company was driving north on West Street, kicking up dust as it approached. John had a big orange patch on the front of his helmet indicating that he was a proby. The officer of the engine company saw an unsupervised proby and stopped his rig and leaned out of his window and ordered John to get on. The officer said that they needed to find water, they needed all the help they could get. John rode to the river with that engine company and began to help stretch hose lines with the others.

Ted and I stopped and leaned on the side of a car. A paramedic appeared; he was tall and thin and coughing uncontrollably. I took two quick breaths from the mask then turned on the purge valve so that a steady flow of air hissed out. I held the face piece up to the paramedic's face. "Just breathe normally. It's air."

The paramedic held the face piece with both hands and breathed for a while and then slowly let it go and leaned over and gripped his knees with his hands. I handed the face piece back to Ted, who was also hunched over holding his knees. The dust was so thick it was difficult to keep our eyes open. I couldn't tell if the rumbling, collapsing noise was still happening or if it had stopped. We stayed there for a while, sharing the mask; it felt like it was impossible to move. I was worried about the ambulance carrying Danny. I tried to picture where they were when the first collapse occurred, but I just couldn't think straight, couldn't place them and I didn't know what had collapsed, which building or how much of it.

We were standing on an incline and the paramedic said, "I think we're in the entrance to the tunnel." After some amount of time, we slowly began to move back into the street and the paramedic continued on his way. Ted said, "stay safe" or something like that and then we headed back toward the rig.

"Where should we go?" a man cried out; he was helping another man. They were stepping through the dust and the papers like they were stepping through snow. We told them they had to go, to get out of the area, to head south. They were the last civilians we would see for the next few hours.

When we got back to the rig, two cops were leaning against it. They were coughing and having trouble standing. Ted took out the EMS bag again. We were out of sterile water, so Ted got some water from the red cooler strapped to the side of Engine 216, the cooler filled with drinking water and ice. He used the water and four by four bandages to clean the police officers' eyes and nose and face.

More cops were staggering towards us and Ted helped the police officers that had just survived the collapse, and they helped themselves. They used the water and rinsed their eyes and mouth and nose. Other than the small group of us it was quiet and deserted. To the north it looked like a wasteland, a nightmare, unrecognizable. Visibility was less than a block and white sheets of paper skidded along the ground and got stuck in the trees and bunched up in corners. I was numb, my mind blank. Ted would do anything I asked. Part of me wanted to leave, just leave the whole fucking thing behind, not have the planes fly into the towers; no one jumping out of windows; not have Danny Suhr get hit; nothing collapsing; all of us back on the rig; driving back over the river to Brooklyn. I wanted to be able to breathe again, to be able to see.

My body shook with the aftereffects of the adrenalin. I was shot. I looked ahead and thought about the ambulance again, and how they probably didn't make it. Ted was covered in white; eyes blood shot, just finishing with the last cop. If I said, 'We need to go to the hospital and check on Danny,' he would have jumped at the chance. But we both knew what we were going to do. "Let's head back."

We walked north, the air starting to clear, the dust starting to settle, bits of blue sky beginning to appear again. But each step we took the dust got deeper. We were near the location of the original Command Post, West and Albany, when a lieutenant and four firefighters gained on us from behind. They were reinforcements, just arriving, fresh and strong. As they rushed past the lieutenant looked at me and said we should hurry, he said that firefighters must be trapped, they need our help.

"We're on our way," I told him. It was difficult to talk and walk at the same time. We were limping on sore feet, blinking sore eyes, coughing, trying to clear our lungs. We kept moving as fast as we could.

I had no idea what had actually happened. I knew there had been two collapses, but hadn't begun to think about the extent of the damage, never once thought that two 110-story buildings were gone, that a total collapse of the Twin Towers had occurred. Even if I had considered it, it would have seemed preposterous. And when I learned that each collapse lasted just over ten seconds, it didn't seem right; it felt so much longer than that. The view now was obscured; it wasn't obvious that both buildings were gone. The degree of the destruction wasn't evident. The horror, the enormity of it, would begin to reveal itself as the day wore on, and I would be as overwhelmed as everyone else by the scope of it. And just like everyone else, even when I finally knew what happened, I still couldn't wrap my mind around it; it was just too big.

A chief appeared in front of us, shell-shocked, dust covered. He wore a white helmet, blue work pants and dress shoes. His turnout coat was open. Fires were burning behind him, just to the north; smoke pouring into the air along with the dust. He was alone. "We have no water!" he said. He had a look in his eyes, desperation; urgency; dread. And determination. He was regrouping, forcing himself to act, taking charge. "We need water!"

The lieutenant and I looked at each other and he and the four firefighters with him rushed off and were soon out of sight. Ted and I walked as quickly as we could, to find a hydrant, to get some water. We went back to the rig, and as we pulled away from the divider on West Street, an officer of a truck company and his five firefighters hurried past, almost jogging toward the collapse. We drove north, made a left on Rector Place and a right on the next block, South End Avenue, and drove north another block or so.

"Let's try one of these," I said. We were a couple of blocks south of Liberty Street; it would be a good place to hook up. Ted unscrewed the cap off the large outlet on the hydrant, put the wrench on the operating nut on top, turned it clockwise and got nothing, no water. I climbed onto the back step; I was going to begin pulling off the three-and-a-half-inch hose we would need to supply water to the site. A red tarpaulin covered the hose bed, secured by elastic straps. I tried to remove one of the straps from the hook that it was fastened to. I looked at my hands as if they didn't belong to me. My fingers didn't have the strength or the coordination to remove the elastic band from its hook. I couldn't believe it.

Ted walked south a block or two and tried four more hydrants; there was no water in any of them. I climbed off the back step and got behind the wheel and drove the rig to his location. I got out and moved into the officer's seat and Ted got in. I wanted to let the chiefs know that the water main on South End Avenue was dead. That another source of water would be needed. I pictured an active Command Post with a command board, with legal pads and lists of companies and sketches and diagrams, the chiefs keeping track of operating units and formulating a plan of attack. I figured they would mark South End Avenue as having no water. They would give us orders as to where to try next, like we were still just fighting a fire. I depressed the button on the microphone of the handie-talkie. "Engine Two-Sixteen to Command Post."

67

There was no response. A fifth alarm had been transmitted for each tower. That's hundreds of firefighters, dozens of chiefs, special units, rescue companies, Field Communications, the Commissioner's Liaison, the Chief of Department.

"Engine Two-Sixteen to Command Post," I repeated. There was nothing but silence. Silence. The hairs on the back of my neck stood up. How was it possible that no one heard that transmission?

Chapter 11

WATER

WE WERE in the rig, Ted behind the wheel, and we heard the roar of a jet flying overhead. It grew louder and closer and more ominous. We looked at each other, ducked, and looked out the windows. There was only blue sky above; the jet had already flown out of sight.

A voice came over the department radio. *"Marine Six to Manhattan. Be advised we're at the foot of Liberty Street. We're ready to supply water. There are no Engines here at this time."*

"Manhattan to Marine Six, 10-4."

"Let's head to the river, find the fireboat," I said. We went west on Rector Place and stopped at the curb of a sidewalk that was protected by concrete planters. The planters had small trees inside of them. We might be able to squeeze through, but we didn't want to get stuck, and we weren't sure if this led to a clear path to the Hudson River. I got out of the rig to take a look.

As I stepped onto the sidewalk, I thought I heard a "Mayday" transmitted over the department radio. I couldn't hear who gave it or what it was for. My first reaction was that someone had made a mistake. The FDNY is very clear as to how and why to give a mayday. It cannot be given over the department radio, the radio on the rig, it is only transmitted on the handie-talkie, the portable radio that firefighters carry.

And it is only used for one of five very specific reasons, a building that is in imminent danger of collapse; a building that has collapsed; a firefighter with a life-threatening injury; a firefighter who is trapped; or a firefighter who is missing or lost. My first reaction should have been to listen, to find out who was in trouble, their location, how we could help. But I was disoriented, overwhelmed, I thought it must be a mistake. The dispatcher began to acknowledge the message but I was already moving away from the rig; I wanted to find the fireboat.

When I got to the Hudson I saw the fireboat about three blocks north, tied up to the bulkhead along the river. It was pitching and rolling in the strong current. I called Ted on the handie-talkie and waved and motioned to him to try to make it. Ted maneuvered the rig through the impossibly tight obstacles; he jumped a curb, squeezed through a few sets of planters, jumped another curb, through more barriers and headed towards the water. I got in and we made a right turn and raced north on the cobblestone esplanade along the river; an esplanade that might not even support the weight of a rig. Just before we reached the fireboat another engine company pulled up from the street side and stopped directly in front of the boat. We turned right and stopped about a hundred feet away, facing east.

Dust covered the street and benches, it covered the trees and low concrete walls, and it coated the turnout gear and the faces of the firefighters. We walked up to the fireboat. A group of firefighters were stretching a three-and-a-half-inch hose line from the fireboat to the pumper that had just pulled up. Ted joined them. Once the hose line from the fireboat was hooked up to the rig, they began to stretch another three-and-a-half-inch line from the pumper toward the site.

I walked ahead of them. When I got to the first intersection, South End Avenue and Albany Street, I looked in all four directions and saw no other rigs. I was about to call Ted, to have him bring our rig to the intersection, when an engine company raced up and stopped. I spoke to the lieutenant and we agreed that he would use his rig to stretch the next six lengths of hose. He would first stretch the hose then bring his rig back to the intersection. The hose that was already being stretched from the engine company near the fireboat would be connected to his rig. We were setting up a relay. The relay was standard operating procedure in the FDNY for supplying water long distances. A pumper was required every six lengths of hose, about 300 feet, to pump and provide an adequate volume of water. We would use as many engines as needed to reach the site.

Meanwhile another hose line was being stretched from the fireboat, a five-inch supply line. It was a large diameter hose designed to have minimal friction loss so that it could supply water nearly unlimited distances. It could be stretched straight to West Street, four or five blocks from the Hudson River, and would provide a tremendous amount of water. It could be used to supply an engine company, and along with the three-and-a-half-inch hose from the relay, two good sources of water would be available on the south side of the site. At least that was the plan that was developing.

As everyone pulled the hose, more firefighters ran up and joined in to help. They were wearing an odd assortment of fire gear, shorts and turnout coats or long pants and T-shirts; some wore helmets; some just a baseball cap; and the dust quickly whitened their black boots and shoes and sneakers. We didn't know it at the time, but the Fire Department had instituted a total recall of all off-duty personnel. Firefighters from all over the city were coming in and going to work. It was a challenge for all of us to work together. The large five-inch hose was heavy and would get snagged periodically as it was dragged towards West Street. Then it would have to be reversed, maybe pulled back a few feet, before it could continue.

I saw Danny Williams, a lieutenant in Ladder Company 16. We had known each other for nearly 20 years, were firefighters together in

Ladder Company 22. He was busy pulling hose, working three or four firefighters behind me on the line, maybe 30 feet away. The advance of the hose line stopped for a moment and we approached each other and hugged. I was so glad to see him—neither of us spoke—we just stood in the street and embraced.

Danny was one of the good guys. He had been in Vietnam, had got on the job in 1977, the tail end of the 'war years' in the FDNY, the late 60's into the 70's, a time of social unrest and an extraordinary amount of fire duty. Vast sections of the city burned, from Brooklyn to Queens to the Bronx, from Staten Island to Manhattan. When I was a proby in Engine 76 and Ladder 22, many of the senior firefighters had been on the job during the war years and they had a tremendous amount of experience as a result. But Danny wasn't just an excellent firefighter; he was also a generous, kind-hearted, decent, honest man—one of the best. He would give you the shirt off his back. Seeing him somehow brought me out of the nightmare, just for a moment.

He and the members of Ladder 16 had also responded to the fifth alarm for Two World Trade Center. He would tell me many years later that while they were waiting for an assignment at the Command Post on West Street, many people were jumping out of the windows from the upper floors of One World Trade Center, the north tower. The sight shook the members of his company. Danny told them to stop watching, to say a prayer; there was nothing else they could do. Then the members of Ladder 16 were caught in both collapses. They had been subjected to that ungodly sound and somehow survived the falling steel and the wind and the dust.

Most of the firefighters coming in from home didn't have equipment, including radios, but Danny had one and so did I. We spaced ourselves apart, maybe two blocks or so, to help coordinate the stretch. He headed towards the buildings and I went back towards the river.

A battalion chief stood on the esplanade by the boat taking charge of the effort to supply water. He was wearing a white shirt, dark pants, old rubber boots and a white helmet. The firefighters grabbed the hose and pulled it forward. Danny called me on the radio; we needed to stop, to back up a bit, to start again. Dust hung in the air, kicked up by the constant motion of the firefighters, and there was also smoke, a haze, all around us. To the east the dust may have been starting to settle and the view was becoming a little more distinct. There was a rumor that more planes were heading our way. I looked up at the sky, but it was empty, a vibrant blue. Yet even though there wasn't a cloud in the sky, no sunshine seemed to make its way down to the street. It was as if we were working at dusk or twilight.

At one point I saw that John Johnson was working alongside Ted. The engine company that had plucked him off West Street after the second collapse had stopped near the fireboat and John jumped off and started to help. We pulled the hose and limped forward. We were pulling against the weight of the hose and pulling against the weight of what had happened. I kept thinking about Danny Suhr. I also kept trying to picture where the ambulance might have been when the collapse occurred. I wanted to call the hospital, or the firehouse, but there was no time. We needed to help get water to the fire.

Radio transmissions on the handie-talkies were starting to increase. Chiefs, company officers and individual firefighters were involved in rescues. There was a short series of transmissions where a firefighter was lost, then found, and then removed. Captain Ralph Tiso and incoming members of Rescue 3 were actively searching the collapse pile, "The Pile", the first time I heard that word. I hadn't even seen it yet. The pile was the term firefighters would use for the next several months when referring to the vast debris field left behind after the World Trade Center complex was destroyed. It sounded like Rescue 3 had climbed to some nearly untenable location, searching for victims, and were now calling for a hose line to help push back fire so they could get back to safety. It sounded like they were desperately trying to rescue anyone they could and had put their lives in mortal danger in the process. Al Fuentes was trapped in his car or near his car and members were in contact with him and helping him. He might have given the mayday I heard earlier. And years later I learned that civilians had given maydays over the department radio. It was all unprecedented, beyond comprehension.

There were now engine companies placed every three hundred feet or so, relaying water from the Hudson River to the site. Two separate engine companies were out on West Street, between Liberty Street and Albany Street, near the original Command Post. The three-and-a-half-inch hose from the relay supplied one engine company and the five-inch hose directly from the fireboat supplied the other. A third line was being stretched, another three-and-a-half-inch relay. It was difficult to say how long it took to get a good supply of water; it was over an hour, maybe two. But water was flowing now and chiefs were getting organized, assigning engines and trucks to different tasks. There were at least fifty firefighters between the river and West Street, maybe a hundred. I was having trouble breathing and my head was pounding. I needed water. I found Ted and John and told them we were going to take a blow, fire department terminology for a break, a short rest.

We took off our helmets and gloves and coats and placed them on the rig. Someone handed us a gallon jug of water. We slumped down on the ground and leaned against a concrete retaining wall near the river. We drank from the jug and splashed water on to our heads and into our eyes. There was nothing to say. We had met only a few hours ago, may have lost a man, a very good man, and possibly more. We had been caught in two collapses, worked at a sprint, and now sat and stared at the Hudson River as it flowed by. We stared at New York harbor, wide open to the sea. The sun reflected off the chop and we looked out at the water and at the blue sky that seemed endless. The scene would be considered beautiful, even peaceful, under normal circumstances. But there was no comfort for anybody, no beauty, no peace.

The fireboat floated nearby, the diesel engines pulsing, driving the pumps that supplied the river water through the hoses to the site. The engine company closest to the fireboat also pumped water, and black smoke pushed out of the exhaust pipe near the rear tires. I pictured the scene when we arrived, Chief Barbara standing at the Command Post, calm and focused. He was working through the problem, prioritizing, confident, unfazed by the enormity of the challenges in front of him, the fire; the evacuation; the gathering of resources; their utilization; how best to save as many lives as possible. I pictured the engine company near the south pedestrian bridge extinguishing a burning car, or maybe it was part of the plane or the building. I pictured Danny Suhr. Especially Danny Suhr. I rubbed my eyes and tried to picture it differently, tried to change it from happening.

After a few minutes we stood and retrieved our gear from the rig. My feet were raw from running in boots that are made for firefighting, not for running. We put the coats and helmets back on; they were wet and heavy.

"Do you have masks?" I asked.

"I'll find one," Johnson answered. He looked rested, ready for more.

"Mine's gone," Ted said. His eyes were bloodshot; he spoke slowly.

"Okay, no masks. They'll be plenty to do without them," I said. We started to walk east on Albany Street, toward the buildings. White papers lay everywhere, hundreds of documents scattered on the ground, maybe thousands, invoices; lists; letters; reports. I picked one up; it had the letterhead of a financial firm on top, names in a column down the left side and rows of numbers printed alongside the names from left to right.

We made a left on South End Avenue and walked to the rear entrance of the Winter Garden. The Winter Garden was a ten-story atrium located across West Street from the World Trade Center, an arched structure, with a roof made out of thousands of panels of glass. Office workers ate lunch sitting on the steps inside the Winter Garden on a normal day, flooded in natural light. Now a hose line was stretched through the rear door, it was charged, filled with water. Café tables and chairs sat outside, empty, covered in dust. The sun shone bright onto the plaza between the Winter Garden and the river. A fireboat was docked and pumping a few blocks north. It wasn't the same fireboat we had worked with down on Liberty Street, but a second boat, supplying water to the north side of the site.

We followed the hose line that went through the rear door, using a flashlight in the dark building. The structure was not in good shape. The roof was heavily damaged, broken glass panels hung from the steel framework above and chunks of concrete and pieces of structural steel lay on the floor. Some chairs and tables were still standing in their normal positions, but most were knocked over or crushed. Water flowed from somewhere and daylight showed at numerous cracks in the wall to the east—the wall facing the towers. We walked through a long corridor, stepped over crushed cardboard boxes and broken wooden pallets. Water covered the floor. The hose line passed through an opening and led outside. We stopped dead in the opening, the scene stunned us; it looked like the end of civilization.

Chapter 12
THE HOSPITAL

WHEN JOHN Johnson had closed the doors of the ambulance carrying Danny Suhr, it headed north. And then it made a U-turn and headed south. Manhattan is an island, eleven miles long, narrow at the northern and southern tips, and nearly two miles wide at its widest point. The widest part of the island corresponds roughly to the area from 14th Street to 23rd Street, and Bellevue Hospital is on 23rd Street. It's on the east side of Manhattan, overlooking the East River. On a normal day the quickest route from the World Trade Center to Bellevue Hospital would've been to head south around the tip of Manhattan then north up the east side to 23rd Street. And this was not a normal day.

Emergency vehicles were converging on the area, two thousand NYPD and Port Authority police officers, more than 100 EMS ambulances plus dozens of private ambulances, over two hundred FDNY units, all of them with lights and sirens, all of them with the right of way. If the ambulance carrying Danny Suhr had tried to head against the crush of responding vehicles, they likely would not have gotten far. But they made the wise choice and headed south.

The NYPD highway cop led the way. They raced down West Street, nearly empty, through the Battery Park Underpass, emerging on the east side and now flying north on the FDR Drive. Inside the ambulance

Tony Sanseviro, Chris Barry and the EMT, Richard Erdy, worked non-stop, performing CPR while bumping and bouncing through the potholes. It's difficult to look out of the windows of an ambulance, and they were probably in the underpass or already heading up the Drive when the south tower collapsed, so they didn't know it happened. Even if they could've seen it, all three of them were so focused on trying to revive Danny that they wouldn't have been aware of anything else. So they drove around the tip of Manhattan and up the east side, consumed with the tragedy in front of them, unaware that the horror they had left behind was now unimaginably worse.

The ambulance pulled up at the emergency entrance of Bellevue Hospital and Chris Barry described a crowd of men and women standing and waiting: doctors; nurses; interns; residents; administrators; social workers; security guards; trauma teams; orderlies; aides; on duty and off duty. They were standing next to stretchers; standing in the corridors; wearing scrubs and gowns and civilian clothes; crash carts ready. Routine surgeries were canceled—beds emptied. If a patient could walk, they were discharged. Bellevue, NYU, St. Vincent's, and Beekman Downtown activated their highest level of mass casualty incident protocols. But at Bellevue there were very few patients. They rushed Danny into the ER and went to work on him immediately. Bellevue Hospital was the premier trauma center in New York, one of the busiest trauma centers in the world.

They prepped Danny and assessed him and worked on him with all their accumulated expertise and knowledge, with all the best resources available. They worked on him for a long time and did everything they could. After every possibility to revive Danny had been exhausted, Chris and Tony moved to stand alongside the operating table. A priest came in and performed the Anointing of the Sick.

After the first plane flew into the north tower, the regularly assigned captain of Engine Company 216, Ted Jankowski, hurried into the firehouse. When he got there, he learned that Danny Suhr had been seriously injured. Jankowski told Brian Charles to drive to Danny's house, pick up his wife, Nancy, and drive her to Bellevue. Brian was close friends with Danny, they came on the job together and lived near each other. Jankowski told Brian to call Nancy first, to let her know he was coming, and then the captain left the firehouse and rushed to the hospital.

Nancy Suhr was in the butcher shop with her two-year-old daughter, Briana, when the first plane struck the first tower. The butcher had just handed Briana a piece of cheese because, as Nancy said, Briana didn't like salami or any of the other samples that the butcher routinely shared with his customers. Nancy and the man looked at the TV at the end of the counter, at the image of the burning tower, and Nancy looked down at Briana and said, trying to sound lighthearted, but serious, "Daddy's going to have a long day today." The butcher nodded.

Nancy left the store and, on her way home, drove down 138 Street, her old block, the block in Belle Harbor where she and Danny had lived for the first nine years of their marriage. She drove to the end of the block because she knew that there was an unobstructed view of the World Trade Center from there. She was shocked at the amount of smoke pouring from the building; she got home as fast as she could. Her answering machine was blinking and when she played the message it was Danny:

Hey baby, it's me. Just calling to tell you I love you. See you later...

Nancy turned on the TV and saw that a second plane had struck the south tower and both buildings were burning. She called her friend Jackie. Jackie had a child Briana's age and she and Nancy were close friends. While they were on the phone the south tower collapsed. Nancy said, "I told Jackie that Danny was there. I just felt it in my bones that Danny was there."

Brian Charles called and told Nancy that Danny was injured. Nancy asked, "How bad?" and Brian said he didn't know. He told her that he was on his way and that he would take her to the hospital. She called Jackie again and asked her to pick up Briana. She called her parents' house, her father was out, so she told her mother that Danny was hurt, that she was going to the hospital and that Briana would be with Jackie.

It was supposed to be Briana's first day of pre-school, the afternoon session, but soon the school would be closed for the day. Frantic parents were beginning to take their children out of schools all across New York City. Workers were leaving jobs, flights were being grounded, bridges and tunnels closed, and Brian Charles arrived at Nancy's house in Belle Harbor about the same time as Jackie. Jackie took Briana to her house and Nancy went to the hospital to find her husband.

Nancy remembered that Brian never used the air conditioning in his old car and if anyone complained he had a simple response, "Roll down the window." The first thing she noticed when she got in that Tuesday morning was that the AC was on. He wore his uniform. He wasn't sure which streets were open, which routes might be closed, so he had his badge ready as they drove from the Rockaways toward Manhattan. When they got to the Brooklyn-Battery Tunnel, the police weren't letting anyone through. They sat in the car at the entrance to the tunnel. After a short time Brian recognized one of the cops, an old childhood friend. Brian explained who Nancy was and what they were doing, where they were going. An NYPD Emergency Services truck was just passing by, heading into the tunnel. Brian's friend told him to follow the ESU truck, stay on its bumper and don't stop. So Brian drove through the tunnel as close to the truck as possible and when they emerged Nancy couldn't believe the desolation.

She had worked in lower Manhattan for thirteen years. She knew what the area looked like at ten or eleven on a Tuesday morning, but now the sidewalks were deserted, there were no groups of office workers sharing a cigarette in front of their building; no bike messengers racing in and out of the lobbies carrying boxes and bags; no food vendors with lines of hungry customers; there was no traffic, no cars and trucks and cabs. Papers skidded along the empty streets, dust hung in the air, and emergency vehicles were everywhere.

They sped through the Battery Park Underpass and onto the FDR Drive heading north, taking the same route the ambulance had taken perhaps an hour before. There were no other cars on the road. All was lifeless and silent, and that's when it struck her—the enormity of it. Her heart sank, her stomach turned, she felt light-headed and dizzy. She remembers thinking with clarity and certainty that no one survived, no one could have survived a disaster that would make the city look like this. They got to the emergency room at Bellevue Hospital and as they pulled up Nancy saw the same crowd of medical personnel that Chris Barry had described. They were massed and prepared for an onslaught of the injured; they were expectant and waiting.

· · ·

Chris Suhr became a firefighter in 2000, like his father and his brother Dan. He was assigned to Engine Company 280 in Brooklyn but was currently on his rotation in Engine 266 on 92nd Street in Rockaway. On September 11, 2001 Chris Suhr was on vacation and at a little after 9:00 AM he was in a bank in Brooklyn near his apartment. When he left the bank he saw smoke rising over the southern tip of Manhattan and he turned on the radio in his car and heard that two planes had crashed into the World Trade Center. He went to his apartment and had several messages on his answering machine. The messages notified him that a total recall was in effect and that he was to report to his firehouse as soon as possible. He went to Engine 266 and then got on a bus with the other members of his company. They were brought to a staging area in Cunningham Park in Queens. Another bus soon picked them up and dropped them off at the World Trade Center just before the north tower collapsed.

Once the dust started to settle Chris noticed that the firefighters who knew both him and Dan seemed to be avoiding him. If he asked anyone if they had seen Engine 216 or Danny, he would get strange noncommittal responses. He was getting suspicious, and beginning to worry. He was working with the other firefighters, trying to get water to put out the fires, searching, trying to find anyone trapped, when Steve Orr approached. Steve was a childhood friend of Dan and a fellow firefighter. He was with Kevin Gallagher and Dr. Kerry Kelly. Kevin Gallagher was the president of the Uniformed Firefighters Association, the UFA, the labor union that represented the firefighters. Dr. Kelly told Chris that Dan had suffered a blunt trauma injury and had been transported to the hospital. "Is he going to make it?" Chris asked.

Dr. Kelly responded, "I don't know." She also wasn't sure which hospital Dan had been taken to. Steve Orr and Kevin Gallagher got an NYPD squad car to take Chris to the nearest hospital to look for his brother. Steve took it upon himself to stay with Chris and they drove in the squad car first to one then another and then another hospital with no luck. Bellevue was the fourth or fifth hospital they tried. When they pulled up and asked one of the staff members out front if a firefighter, Daniel Suhr, had been taken there, they were told simply, "Yes, Daniel Suhr is here."

Greg Rupp met Chris as he entered the hospital and he and Steve Orr walked with Chris down a long corridor, one on each side of him. Greg Rupp was close to Dan, had played football with him for the FDNY, and was devasted. The corridor went on and on and they walked in silence until finally Chris stopped and faced Gregg Rupp, "Okay, what the hell's going on? Just tell me." And that's when they told him. Dan had died. Chris doesn't remember much after that. Dan was his older brother; he was the one with the plans, the FDNY; football; N&D Pizza. Chris remembers just a few days prior that he and Dan were trying to replace the lock in a door in their parents' house. One of the screws was loose and they laughed as they remembered how their father had told them that if you stick a little splinter of wood in the hole, the screw will "grab." But as large as Chris's fingers were, Dan's were even larger and they couldn't quite manipulate the little piece of wood into the hole. And that was the last time Chris saw Dan alive.

After Chris spent some time with the body of his brother, Brian Charles drove him home. Brian had driven Nancy to the hospital, but Chris doesn't remember seeing her at Bellevue. He got home and made some phone calls. His parents were in Oregon visiting his brother Ed and his family. His sister Lee lived in Virginia. By the time the day turned into night he had made his way to Nancy's house.

• • •

Chris Barry said that when Captain Jankowski arrived at Bellevue, the captain told him and Tony that both buildings had collapsed. They couldn't believe it. They all felt there was a good chance that everybody from 216 had perished. Tony and Chris wanted to go back to the site, but Captain Jankowski wouldn't let them. He ordered them to go to the firehouse. In two days they would all be there together, but for now, Jankowski wasn't going to let them go back down.

Chris Barry remembered when Nancy Suhr arrived at the hospital, "I couldn't face her, could barely look her in the eye. I felt so guilty to be alive, that Danny was gone." When Nancy saw Chris, he was standing against a wall on the far side of the room and his face was gray, ashen.

As Nancy began to walk into the emergency room, she saw Captain Jankowski standing in the doorway of a room. He made eye contact. He approached her deliberately, solemnly, respectfully and said, "I'm

83

so sorry Nancy." He would later describe the lasting impression of that fateful moment: "I had to do what every fire officer fears, telling a family member that their loved one was not coming home. That Dan died bravely and heroically in the line of duty." Nancy leaned against a wall and slumped slowly to the floor. She sat for a minute with her head in her hands and Captain Jankowski helped her to her feet.

She looked him in the eyes, "Who's going to walk her down the aisle? What about her first holy communion?" Nancy asked—choking back tears, wondering about all the special moments that would never be the same.

Captain Jankowski said, "We'll figure it out." Nancy felt like she had had a premonition of his death; she knew him, knew he would do whatever it took to help. If people were in trouble Danny was going to try to get to them. That's who he was. She felt like she knew it all along.

Nancy couldn't go in to see him yet, and a social worker appeared. The social worker and Captain Jankowski walked with her, holding her arms on either side, supporting her. But she didn't want to be supported, she wanted to be alone for a minute. She said she had to use the restroom. She stood in the bathroom and told herself not to faint, not to pass out; she had fainted before, and Danny always knew exactly what to do to help her. She realized who she needed right then, she needed Danny. She needed her husband to help her get through this. She was brought to an office and was sitting with the social worker and after some time Nancy wondered out loud, "What do I do now?"

The woman answered, "Maybe you can call someone?"

The first person Nancy called was her sister Luanne. When Luanne answered Nancy said simply, "He's gone." Years later Nancy learned that Luanne was sitting at her desk at work as they were speaking, that Luanne had turned white, so pale that her co-workers in the office rushed to her aid. But to Nancy she sounded calm and strong and reassuring.

"How can I help?" Luanne asked. Nancy told her that Briana was with Jackie; Nancy wanted to make sure that Luanne knew where Briana was. The second call she made was to her parents. Her father hadn't got home yet so she told her mother. Next, she called her mother-in-law in Oregon, Sheila Suhr. When Sheila answered the phone she asked, "Who's hurt, Chris or Dan?" And Nancy told her that they had lost Danny. Sheila was devastated, and stranded in Oregon, with no way to get home, isolated, separated, in shock. Soon two of Danny's childhood friends, Ricky and John, arrived at the hospital. They had gone to James Madison High School with Danny, their wives were all close, and they offered to drive Nancy to Jackie's house where Briana was. But Nancy wanted to see Danny and after some period of time she was taken to him.

Captain Jankowski held one of her arms and Tony Sanseviro the other as they guided her to the room where Danny was. She wanted to speak to him—so much to say—to tell him that she would take care of Briana, that she would make sure Briana knew her father, what type of man he was. She promised. She lingered for several minutes and then slowly left the room. "I wish I had stayed longer, I always regretted it," she said. "Just a few more minutes." Afterwards, Tony assured her that Danny was never alone, and she finally made peace with it; but it was still a regret.

Tony Sanseviro and Chris Barry left the hospital later in the day, a police car took them back to their firehouse in Williamsburg. When they stepped out of the squad car there were a lot of firefighters gathered there. Firefighters were standing in the firehouse and out front and some were standing in the street. There were active duty members and retired members, firefighters from Engine 216 and Ladder 108 and Battalion 35; they were there because of the recall, there because of the size of the tragedy, there because they loved Danny. Many of them had just attended the retirement party the night before.

Chris Barry threw his gear on the apparatus floor in the back, behind where the rig should have been. He remembers spending a lot of time with Tony, chain-smoking, trying to get through each minute, worried about Nancy, feeling like shit because he was still alive, and, like everyone else, trying to wrap his mind around the fact that both buildings had collapsed, that so many must've been caught in it, that Danny was gone.

Nancy eventually left the hospital with Ricky and John and they drove to Jackie's house, where Briana was. In the car they all remained silent, which was very unusual for Ricky and John; they normally had something to say about everything. They drove through the deserted streets and finally arrived at Jackie's. Nancy got out of the car and saw a small crowd of people inside Jackie's house and on the sidewalk out front. They all grew quiet as Nancy walked toward the front door. Nancy was uncomfortable with the attention. It was an experience that would repeat itself over and over in the days ahead, an experience that she would have to learn to live with.

Briana and the other little kids were running around the living room, laughing, playing. Briana saw her mother and ran up to her. Nancy crouched and put her arms around her daughter and pulled her close. Nancy felt the small body of her two-year-old, sturdy and warm. When she let go Briana stood and looked into her mother's eyes. And in the middle of the crowded room, with all the adults watching and listening, and all of them trying to hold back tears, she asked, "Where's Daddy?"

"He's in heaven with God," Nancy said. The words came out simply, without hesitation.

"Why?" Briana asked.

"Because God needs some good people to help him out," Nancy said. She looked into her daughter's eyes as she spoke. Briana listened closely, carefully considering what her mother had told her, and after what felt like a very long time she turned and began to play with the other children again. Everyone within earshot was weeping.

Ricky and John couldn't believe it. They looked at Nancy, "What the fuck?" they said, raising their arms, shaking their heads. How did she just offer that explanation to her child? So naturally? How did she know what to say? Why did Briana accept it so easily? Nancy said that Briana never really asked where her father was again. Nancy sometimes worried about it, she talked to professionals, to psychologists, and they said that Briana must have processed it, fit it in somewhere. It was part of her reality, her life, a truth to bear, to tolerate, to endure, another fact to face.

Chapter 13

THE PILE

TED MURRAY, John Johnson and I followed the hose line that was stretched from inside the Winter Garden and stepped through the opening and onto the pile. We realized that the opening was a window, but it didn't seem like a window, it felt like a door. How could someone step directly out of a window on to the ground? The dust had settled enough to see for the first time that the towers were gone; they had disappeared, were no longer standing, they had collapsed, entirely, totally, completely. It was difficult to comprehend, to wrap the mind around, to believe. And yet there it was.

The scene was one of destruction so absolute that it was indescribable, the area of wreckage too large for words, too high and wide, too vast. In the days and weeks to come engineers and FEMA forensic scientists would try to quantify it, in acres; in square footage; in city blocks; in hundreds of thousands of tons of concrete and steel; in KIPS; in the pressure the Hudson River was exerting on the foundation; in the temperature of the fires burning deep below grade level. But in those first moments it was unimaginable.

Firefighters operated everywhere. Engine companies used hose lines hundreds of feet away from each other, to the north and the south, pouring water on fires that were burning on top of the pile, and beneath. Truck companies picked their way over and under the debris, searching for survivors. A forty-seven-story high-rise building to the north, Seven World Trade Center, had smoke pushing out of the lower fifteen floors.

We walked forward, to the east, and looked down as we walked. I shined the beam of my flashlight into the darkness below the twisted steel. We climbed and walked and tried to look beneath the debris and after about twenty minutes saw a hint of red maybe fifteen feet below the surface. We climbed down and squeezed lower and lower to try to see if the glint of red could possibly be what it looked like.

It didn't seem right. The level of the pile got higher to the east; the highest places probably where the twin towers had stood. But the area between the main pile and the Winter Garden was also high, impossibly high. It seemed like we were standing on a building, but if the red below us was what we thought it might be—a fire truck—we must have been standing in the street. We finally got deep enough and saw the diamond plate of the running board. My God. It *was* a rig. Buried fifteen or twenty feet beneath enormous steel beams and rubble.

We got as close as we could and the flashlight illuminated the inside of the cab of the crushed fire truck. It was empty. We tried to climb beneath it, to take a look, but it was flattened too close to the ground. We climbed back up into the bright afternoon light. Daniel Nigro, the Chief of Operations, the second highest-ranking member of the FDNY on September 11th, was climbing out onto the pile. He was moving away from the window with the hose line, the same window we had used. His face was pale and his eyes were red. A truck company, possibly Ladder 126 from Queens, followed close behind.

"Chief, there's a rig down here," I said. Ted and John stood on the surface but I hadn't fully emerged yet and stood chest deep in the rubble and the chief looked down at me as I spoke.

Chief Nigro paused, then turned to face the captain of the truck company. "You can start here," he said. But when he turned he didn't just look over his shoulder, he didn't merely turn his head, he rotated his entire upper body, stiff, slow, measured. He looked devastated, incredulous, in shock. The chief turned and kept climbing, taking tired, determined steps toward the companies in the distance. He was tall and thin and visibly shaken as he advanced slowly into the absolute oblivion to the east. By nightfall he would be promoted to Chief of Department, to replace Chief Peter Ganci who had been killed in the collapse of the north tower. Chief Nigro would be in charge of the FDNY for the next year as the department tried to rebuild from the unprecedented losses. He, like so many others, was forced to confront nearly insurmountable challenges, both personal and institutional, and he, also like so many others, did a remarkable job. The firefighters from Ladder 126 began scrambling over and under the steel to get to the rig below.

I was standing back on the surface as the captain of Ladder 126 moved past me. "I didn't see anyone," I said. The FDNY is clear about responsibilities, and the Chief of Operations had just ordered the captain to search the rig buried below us, so he climbed down with his firefighters to take a look for himself. I saw Danny Williams again, out on the pile in the distance with members of Ladder Company 16; they were walking, climbing, searching. Smoke was pouring from every window of the lower two thirds of Seven World Trade Center now and even the upper floors were beginning to show signs of smoke seeping out of them. An office building over forty stories tall with fire burning on numerous floors would have normally triggered a massive response from the FDNY. But there was no water in the hydrants. There were no rigs and hose and masks, there were no firefighters or company officers to spare, and no chiefs available to supervise them.

We followed the hose line back through the Winter Garden. It was attached to a three-way gate about one hundred feet from the window. If we could've gotten four or five lengths of hose and a nozzle, we would have been able to stretch a line from the unused outlet of the three-way gate. We would be able to put some water on one of the fires out on the pile. Ted and John went to look for the equipment and when they returned they had three lengths of rolled up 1 ¾ inch hose and we made our way inside the building. We still didn't have a nozzle. We began going through the tight hallway again when two engine companies appeared, eight firefighters and two officers, ready to go to work. Each member carried a length of 2 ½ inch hose and the officers told me they had been ordered to stretch a line from the three-way gate to a specific location out on the pile. I told my guys to forget it, the assigned units had the proper size hose, the correct nozzle, they had orders; they would attach their hose to the outlet and operate on the pile. We made our way back outside.

"Cap, can we get in touch with the hospital or something and find out about Danny?" Ted asked.

"Let's get a phone somewhere," I said.

We walked back on to the plaza between the Winter Garden and the river. Boats were docked in the cove, expensive looking yachts gently rocking in the sunshine, tied tightly to stainless steel cleats on wooden piers. I looked for a pay phone and was still looking when John and Ted walked up and Ted shook his head. He had tears in his eyes as he spoke to me, "Danny's gone. Captain Jankowski's at the hospital."

"I'm so sorry Teddy," I said. "The ambulance made it? The other guys are okay?"

"Yeah. They made it." He could barely speak. He held his forehead with one hand and as he stood in the sunshine tears filled his eyes. John's eyes reddened. I felt like I'd been hit with a baseball bat. My head ached. I tried to concentrate, to focus. Chris and Tony made it. But I pictured Danny lying in the street. We walked south, aimlessly.

"Can we go back to the firehouse?" Ted asked.

"Sure. Go down to the river, get the rig. I'll go talk to somebody, get us out of here," I said. Ted and John walked slowly south, passing firefighters who rushed north towards the collapse. It all felt so personal, so tragic, so final. Until we confirmed it, there had still been some hope, even just a little bit, but now it was over.

I made my way back to West Street, north of Liberty Street, just north of the south pedestrian bridge. A group of firefighters looked out on the pile, hoping to get out there, to help, to look for survivors, to do something. Some stood together as companies, others alone as individuals. They were from Queens and Staten Island and the Bronx, there were firefighters from Manhattan and Brooklyn. Some wore full sets of bunker gear with masks and full complements of tools while others wore shorts or a helmet or maybe a turnout coat and carried a Halligan or a hook or an old ax. I spotted a deputy chief from the 11th Division, the division I was assigned to three days prior.

"Chief, I'm with Two-Sixteen. We lost a guy; I'm down to two men, the chauffeur and a proby. Any chance we can get out of here?"

"What?"

"One of my guys got injured and two firefighters from Two-Sixteen went with him to the hospital. He didn't make it. My chauffeur is a good friend. He's pretty beat up. It's just a proby and me. We'd like to take up."

He was busy, swamped, chiefs and company officers waited to talk to him, someone called him on his radio. But he took the time to consider the request, to concentrate on it, and after a long pause he looked into my eyes as he answered, "I'm sorry for your loss, Cap, and your men. Go down by the river. Take a blow; take as much time as you need. But we can't release anyone right now."

I walked away, heading south on South End Avenue, shuffling through the dust and papers. I couldn't believe he had said no. Didn't he realize one of my men was dead? At the corner of South End Avenue and Albany Street, Engine Company 216 sat pumping. Two three-and-a-half-inch hose lines from the Fireboat were supplying it and a three-and-a-half-inch line came off it heading toward the towers. Ted was monitoring the pumps, red-eyed. I stood next to him. "They won't let us leave, not yet anyway. They can't release anyone."

"That's all-right Cap," he said. He focused on the gauges, the volume and pressure and temperature.

"Did you move the rig?"

"No. Someone else must've moved it. And hooked it up. I told him I'm the chauffeur of 216; that I got it. He left a minute ago."

"Okay. Very good," I said. Ted was working, operating, doing his job.

"Before the other guy left, I followed the line to see who we're supplying. It's Engine 207, on West Street," Ted said.

I looked toward the site, toward the smoke, and I regretted asking to be released. Of course we couldn't leave. But it was all too much to think about; both towers gone; the silence on the radio; the dazed look of the chief looking for water; the dust; Danny Suhr; the snatches of conversation and rumors; "Chief Ganci is gone." "So is Chief Downey." "Has anybody seen 40 Engine?" "They bombed the Pentagon...and the White House." The enormity of the loss hadn't set in yet. Somehow, I hadn't really begun to comprehend how many might have perished. I heard that Dr Kelly was missing. And it turned out to be just another rumor, she had actually survived. But still, it was especially jarring. Bill Whelan from Engine 216 approached. We embraced.

"I'm sorry," I said. Bill shook his head, spread his arms as if to say this was beyond all of us. There was no blame to place, and no consolation to be had.

Ted said, "Hey Cap. The rig's running hot." He was standing at the pump panel, looking concerned; the rig was starting to overheat.

Chapter 14

THE CHAUFFEUR

BILL WHELAN joined Ted Murray at the pump panel. They said there wasn't enough water flowing, that's why the rig was running hot. We could try the deck pipe, just to get more water moving through the pumps; it might cool it down. The deck pipe is mounted on top of the rig, just behind the roof of the cab. I told John Johnson to climb up and operate it while Ted opened the gate to supply the water. John directed the nozzle so that the stream of water blasted harmlessly into the street. I wanted to check on the company we were supplying, Engine 207, to see how many lines they had stretched off their rig, where the hose lines were located, to see if anybody would be in a bad spot in case we had to shut down. It was too much for the handie-talkie, the radio was too busy, so I told Ted I was going to go to Engine 207 and talk to the chauffeur while they worked on the rig.

I followed the hose line as it snaked alongside several other hoses in the street. It lay in the dust and papers and the closer it got to the towers, the more steel and rubble it lay on. I headed east; each step was slow, heavy. When I got to West Street and looked north, I was shocked once again by the immensity of it; smoke was rising from the mountains of rubble. West Street was impassable. Massive I-beams were intertwined and twisted. There were thick layers of dust, the white papers skidding everywhere. Further north, smoke rose out of several locations and buildings—fresh smoke—untouched by water. In the distance, smoke was now pushing out of every window on every floor of Seven World Trade Center.

The twenty-three-story building across the street, 90 West Street, had fire on several floors and was heavily damaged. The scaffolding and the sidewalk shed on the west side of the building, facing West Street, were still standing somehow. But the scaffolding and the sidewalk shed on the north side of the building, that had faced Two World Trade Center, where we took refuge while we worked on Danny, was gone. I followed the supply line into the street and past several groups of firefighters, clustered on West Street, between Liberty and Albany. There were three or four chiefs, at about the same location as the original Command Post, but I didn't see Chief Barbara. A chief would call for an engine company or a ladder company. The firefighters would rush forward when called, then head north into the vast collapse zone or head across the street toward 90 West Street.

The chief officers who had taken control were identifying each other by name, not unit designation, which would be the normal means of identification. Their voices came over the handie-talkie, "Chief Fellini to Chief Visconti, do you need another truck company at your location?" "Chief Visconti to Chief Fellini, 10-4. And send two more engines with roll-ups." I followed the hose line through the opening in the center divider on West Street and looked over to where we had been just hours ago, before the collapse. I pictured crossing the street, the rubbish fires and the debris. I pictured Danny Suhr.

I followed the line down Albany Street and found Engine 207. Engine Company 207 was a Satellite Unit, a special unit equipped with a 2,000-gallon per minute pumper that could handle supplying water to multiple hose lines. The chauffeur of Engine 207, Steve Ferriolo, said that he was supplying the standpipe of 90 West Street. He was also supplying two hand lines—one went north on Washington Street towards the pile and the other was stretched about a block and a half away. Steve told me that there was a medium fire condition in the basement of a building at that location and the companies were trying to gain access now. I told him that we were being supplied by a fireboat, so we had a good source of water, but that we were overheating. I would let him know over the handie-talkie if we needed to shut down. The next day I would learn that all the members of Engine 207 who responded with Steve that morning were missing.

When I made my way back to the rig the firefighters had figured out why Engine 216 was overheating. Ted stood beside Bill Whelan at the pump panel and Bill looked at me as he spoke, "Whoever hooked us up probably left it in Drive when they put it in pumps. We're not supplying what we should be. We're not pumping enough water." With water flowing out of the deck pipe, the temperature wasn't rising anymore, but it wasn't decreasing either. And the amount of water we were pumping to Engine 207 was less than required.

Ted said, "We can shut down, turn off the rig, and let it sit for a minute. Then we'll start over. That might do it."

"Let's try it," I said.

Ted sat in the cab with Bill standing in the street next to him. I radioed Steve Ferriolo of Engine 207 and let him know that 216 needed to shut down for a minute, and to let us know when he was ready. After a few minutes Steve radioed back to tell us they were set. Ted shut down the supply to Engine 207 and turned off the rig. He let it sit for a while. When he started it back up he put the transmission in Neutral and engaged the pumps, and then shifted it into Drive to operate. I let the chauffeur of Engine 207 know that Engine 216 was starting water again, and we looked at the gauges. Water was flowing now and the temperature was holding steady.

Lieutenant Ed Schollmeir from Engine 216 approached. He and Ted embraced, and then we hugged.

"You guys all right?" he asked.

"I don't know," Ted answered. And he walked away.

"He's feeling bad about Danny?"

"Real bad. How are Chris and Tony?"

"They're shot. They're back at the firehouse."

"How about Danny's family? He told me about his daughter yesterday, two or three? God. How's his wife?"

"I don't know. Captain Jankowski's with her at the hospital."

Ted stood in front of the pump panel of the rig, monitoring the pumps. More members of Engine 216 and Ladder 108 were walking up to the rig. I recognized some of them but just didn't know their names. Ted turned to me, "The temperature's going down, Cap."

"Excellent. Do you need a blow, Ted? You want to go down by the river?"

"No, I'm good."

"Shut down the deck gun," I said. The solid stream of water that had been blasting out of the nozzle of the deck pipe began to lose its reach. Soon it was breaking apart and it slowed and became a limp flow and the water splashed on to the roof of the cab and then stopped. John Johnson came down off the rig.

"How're you holding up, John?" I asked.

"Fine, Cap," he said.

"I want you to go down to the river, take a blow. Come back in a half hour or so." John Johnson nodded and headed west, kicking up dust as he walked. I stood next to Ted. "I'm sorry about Danny."

"So am I," he said.

"There's nothing any of us could've done about it. You know?"

"Yeah, well, if he was driving, he'd be standing here. Not me."

"You can't say that. That might not be true. We don't know what would've happened."

"Whatever."

"It's not your fault, Ted. It's not my fault either, it was a God-damned terrorist attack," I said. But I didn't believe it, the way I saw it, it *was* my fault. I was responsible for the firefighters working, just like every officer always is. Ted was blaming himself, and I was blaming myself, and none of it was going to change anything.

Ted looked down at the street for a second. Then he finally raised his blood shot eyes and looked at me. "All right, Cap," he said. He reached out and tapped the round piece of glass that covered one of the pressure gauges on the pump panel. He used the tips of two fingers to do it. It was a gesture we both understood to be useless but was still somehow welcomed, like it could make things seem normal again.

I saw Jack Mooney rushing past us. Jack had been a lieutenant in Engine Company 84 when I was a firefighter in the adjoining company, Ladder 34. Now Jack was a battalion chief. I walked after him and called out. He stopped and turned to face me. "How are you, Paul?"

"I lost a firefighter, Daniel Suhr. I was in Two-Sixteen, we responded to the fifth alarm for Two World Trade Center, he was hit by a jumper on the way in."

"Oh, man, I'm so sorry," he said. And he looked at me for a few moments, shaking his head. Then he continued, "Listen, who did you report in to?"

"Chief Barbara."

"Gerry Barbara," Jack said and he looked down at his feet. He looked up, "Where was the last place you saw him?"

"At the Command Post, at West and Liberty, or West and Albany."

"What did he say? I mean, at the Command Post. What was the last thing you heard him say?"

"We need more guys...As we headed for the building he turned to his aide and said *we need more guys*."

"Yeah, I think he transmitted a second alarm at some point. Thanks. I'm so sorry about Danny Suhr. So many guys. Hang in there, stay safe. I have to go." It was then that I noticed the clipboard he was carrying, a yellow legal pad on it with a list of names written in pencil. He was trying to account for missing members, helping to establish an organized search. He rushed off, heading north.

A group of members from Engine 216 and Ladder 108 gathered nearby. They had lost Danny Suhr, and the strain and the grief of their loss showed on their faces. It weighed on each one of them. And they knew countless others were missing—firefighters and civilians. They were desperate to find someone, anyone, alive. They had just come off the pile and were covered in dust, but they hadn't found anyone yet.

Transmissions over the handie-talkie announced that Seven World Trade Center was going to collapse. Everyone was to stand clear of the area. Firefighters were walking away from West Street, passing Engine 216. I moved closer to the rig and Ted continued to stand by the pump panel and watch the volume of water coming into the rig and the volume of water going out. He continued to watch the pressure and the temperature. He said that the temperature wasn't a problem anymore and the rig was pumping well. But we were down to half a tank of fuel. All the rigs that had been pumping since the beginning would be running out of fuel soon.

Chapter 15

FUEL

I WANTED to let the command post know that we needed fuel. "Engine Two-Sixteen to Command Post," I said over the handie-talkie, but the radio was too busy for my message to get through, the chiefs had too many other messages to deal with.

John Johnson walked up as he came back from the river. "How can I help, Cap?"

"Stay with Ted," I said. "Stick together, I'm going to let them know we're running out of fuel. We're all running low."

I walked north, back to where I had spoken to the deputy chief from Division 11 an hour or two ago. I wanted to try to talk to somebody face to face. There was a staging area of sorts just south of the Winter Garden, north of the pedestrian bridge. There were cases of water stacked nearby, the first evidence of the extraordinary generosity that would be exhibited for the next nine months towards those who were working at Ground Zero. Fifty or so firefighters were gathered there, waiting for an assignment. A group of chiefs were standing nearby discussing strategy. After they were finished, I approached one of them and told him that all the rigs supplying water from the fireboat at Liberty Street were going to need fuel soon. The chief said that they were aware of the problem, it was being addressed. Fuel was going to arrive, but not for at least a few more hours. He advised that the fireboats usually have spare diesel.

Before walking back, I looked at the scene before me. Seven World Trade Center had heavy smoke pushing out of every opening and crack. I learned years later that it had been searched and once it was determined that no civilians were inside, a collapse zone was established around the building and it was monitored, but no further extinguishment efforts would be undertaken. Firefighters climbed and walked and crawled all over the pile. They were surrounded by smoke and dust and the imminent danger of secondary collapse. They looked like an army combing a battlefield in search of survivors. Actually, they were an army combing a battlefield searching for survivors. Everyone had a serious, sad, shocked expression on their dust covered, red-eyed faces. I hobbled back to 216.

"We got less than half a tank, Cap," Ted said.

I turned to the proby. "John, go down to the fireboat and tell them we've got less than half a tank of fuel, that other Engines need diesel too. Give them our location and see if they can help. Let me know what they tell you."

A chief from a fire department in New Jersey approached. He had a list of names and the name of a hospital written on a scrap of paper. He said that there were three New York City firefighters who were injured but alive, and he said they were safe and being cared for in a hospital across the Hudson River. I thanked him and told Ted I would be right back. I walked back to the Command Post on West Street and found a chief who had just sent a group of firefighters out onto the pile. I handed the piece of paper to the chief. "This is a list of firefighters in a hospital in Jersey. They are injured but safe. A chief from over there just gave it to me."

"Thanks Cap. I'll take care of it."

The transmissions over the handie-talkie radios concerning rescues and removals had decreased dramatically. There had been a lot of activity describing people trapped, people removed, and rescue efforts being undertaken. For a few hours it sounded like a lot of civilians would be found, that missing firefighters would be located, Ladder Company 6 had been triumphantly removed from the B stairwell of Tower One. But for the last hour or so, there had been very few messages dealing with rescue operations. I headed back to Engine 216 and stood next to Ted as John Johnson walked up. He looked at both of us as he spoke. "A lieutenant from the boats said he'd try to find some fuel. He said he'd let us know if he can't."

"Good, John. Go check the other rigs and see what they need," I said. He walked to three engine companies that were pumping nearby. The traditional FDNY rule—*at large scale operations take care of your own needs and don't bother the overburdened command structure*—was being followed all over the site. Firefighters and officers and chiefs were improvising and inventing solutions to problems that they had never faced before. No one had ever searched the wreckage of the collapse of a 110-story building. They were searching two of them. When John came back, he said that all three engine companies in our area were down to less than half a tank.

A pick-up truck pulled up with an officer and two firefighters from the Marine Division. They had two 55-gallon drums of diesel fuel in the bed of the truck, but they had no pump to deliver it. Ted suggested a hydrant pump and began looking for one on the rig. It was a good idea. I sent the proby to check the other rigs to see if they had one. After a few minutes he came back. No one had a hydrant pump, but he had found a twenty-foot length of ¾ inch black rubber hose.

The firefighters from the Marine Division began setting up a siphon. They placed one end of the small diameter hose in the opening in the top of the drum of diesel fuel up on the bed of the pickup and one firefighter sucked carefully on the other end. In a short time diesel fuel began to flow from the hose and he jerked his mouth away. "That tastes like shit," he said, spitting the fuel into the street. The other firefighter with him laughed a bit, and we all smiled, just for a moment. He placed the hose into the inlet of the fuel tank on Engine 216 while he wiped his mouth with the back of his sleeve. Ted and John stood by the rig and the Marine Company firefighters held the hose.

There was a constant movement of people past our location, firefighters; police officers; paramedics; EMT's; sanitation workers; construction workers; engineers; city, state and federal, uniformed and civilian. They were kicking up dust as they walked. They headed in all four directions, north, south, east and west. Some were just arriving, seeing the devastation for the first time, others headed toward the river to take a rest, and there were those who were changing locations, trying to find a place where they could be more effective, trying to find a job that needed to be done. Everyone wanted to help. Everyone wanted to find someone, a fellow firefighter or police officer, an EMT or paramedic. They were all looking for civilians. No one knew how many civilians might be missing, but the number was sure to be staggering. It was getting to be late in the afternoon. Several ambulances were parked along South End Avenue, starting at Albany Street, facing south. But none of them had any patients. I looked at Ted. "How much fuel do we have?"

Ted climbed up into the cab, with effort. "A little over half," he answered after checking the fuel gauge. His eyes were red and his words were hollow.

"It's going to take a while," I said. It must've been around 5:00 PM and I wanted to try to call home. I had wanted to call home for hours but there just hadn't been the time, or any way to do it. Most people didn't have cell phones, not most firefighters anyway—my family had one, but six of us shared it. I wanted to call, to speak to my wife, to see if she was all right, to hear her voice, to reconnect, to tell her I loved her.

Mary was a teacher and was working at her school when the first plane flew into the north tower. She tried to call my firehouse but couldn't get through. She tried to call her father, and my mother, both Manhattan residents, but the lines were jammed. And she was concerned about her brother, Paul Geoghegan, who was also a firefighter. She tried to call all day and was growing more worried as the hours went by. But she stayed calm in front of her students and colleagues, and in front of the parents who arrived to pick up their children. She was certain I was there. But somehow, she also knew that I was okay, that I was alive. She was still anxious, and she still kept trying to call, but some part of her felt that I was going to get through it.

When she left work, she met our daughters, Eileen and Kathryn, at St. Francis Prep High School. Our younger children, Margaret and Paul, walked home together from the local elementary school. They all knew something was wrong, something unprecedented and horrendous. Once they were home Mary reassured them, and they prayed. They prayed for me, for the firefighters, and for everyone facing the horror of the day. There were over 30 messages on the answering machine, "Is Paul okay?" "Have you heard anything?" "Are the kids home?" "Can I help?" She skimmed through the messages trying to find the one from me, or from somebody in the Fire Department, some word about what was going on. She tried to remain calm and hopeful.

Mary's brother Paul was working that day in northern Manhattan, in Engine Company 84 in Washington Heights. I had been a firefighter in the same firehouse, in Ladder Company 34, but had been promoted to lieutenant before Paul got there. He tried to track me down. Considering that there was a total recall, that unknown numbers of firefighters were working at the World Trade Center site, that companies were being relocated everywhere, and that chief and company officers were desperately trying to keep track of their firefighters, it wasn't easy for Paul to find out where I was assigned for the day. While not out on calls with Engine 84, he kept working on it, and eventually found out that I was in Engine Company 216. He tried to call several times. He kept getting interrupted, busy signals, no answer. He finally got through late in the afternoon and was given a brief description of what had happened and was told that I had survived. He hung up and called his sister.

Mary felt incredibly relieved when Paul confirmed that I had made it. But the relief only lasted a few seconds and was followed by guilt; followed by the knowledge that untold others wouldn't receive the same good news. She thanked her brother for finding out, for calling— we would always be grateful to him for that.

She told Eileen and Kathryn and Margaret and Paul that I was all right. There was an immediate shift, now they felt the same sorrow that everyone was feeling at the events of the day, but the worry that their father was gone was lifted. Their spirits soared from despair and loss to elation and gratitude. Yet even as they embraced the fact that I had survived, the reality of the day came rushing back, the planes crashing, the buildings collapsing, the clouds of dust, the lost and the missing. And their spirits dropped again.

I was standing next to Engine 216 and about a hundred yards away I saw a young firefighter talking on a cell phone. I walked toward him and as soon as he was done, I asked to borrow it. I felt sorry that it took me so long to find a phone and to call home. I thought about how worried my wife and kids must have been. I took my gloves off and found that it was difficult to make my hands hold the small phone, and to concentrate enough to dial the number. My daughter Kathryn answered, and something about hearing her voice, so innocent and young, made me start to lose my composure, and I paused and said something about a bad connection, trying to conceal how I was feeling. When Mary got on, her voice washed over me like a wave, a wave of love, and of the life we shared for over 20 years. I lost whatever bit of self-control I had left and tears blurred my eyes.

Mary was used to worrying about me, especially during night

tours. She was experiencing the same emotions that everyone else was that long, horrible day, along with the added anxiety of knowing I was there. But she had that belief that I was alive, and she held on to that belief throughout the day, it was real and true. Still, when she heard my voice she experienced an overwhelming sense of gratitude, and even joy. And at the same time she was worried and sad for all our friends, for members of the FDNY family, and every single soul in the towers. Sorrow and joy, both emotions filled both of us simultaneously.

When we finally spoke, we were rushed. I had so much to tell her, and she had so much to tell me, but we knew we didn't have the time. I told her briefly that one of my firefighters had died, and she was heartsick. She couldn't speak for a moment. She said that she would pray for him and his family. She said that she had been praying all day for all of us, for the firefighters, for their families, and for everyone lost and injured and for all their loved ones. What a horrendous day. I told her I would be home, but not until late. Maybe very late. She wished I could leave now, to get away from the destruction, the danger, and she implored me to stay safe. We tried to reassure each other, taking turns at trying to find something to say that felt comforting, but there was so little that could be said. It felt impossible to say goodbye, yet it seemed that as soon as it started, our conversation ended.

After I hung up, I had to stand for a minute, to refocus, to try to regain some composure before I thanked the firefighter who gave me the phone. As he walked away groups of firefighters appeared, they were moving fast, west on Albany Street, away from the site. They were clearly being chased by something. As they passed us, heading for the river, a distant rumbling could be heard. One of them called out, "Seven World Trade Center is coming down."

"*There it goes.*" I believe the words were transmitted over the handie-talkie. We looked and waited for the dust and debris to begin again, ready to run, but it never came. We were too far away from it. I prayed that no one was caught in this third major collapse of the day.

The marine company firefighters were still refueling the rig when Lieutenant Ed Schollmeir approached and reminded me that he was my relief. Lieutenant Schollmeir had been searching and digging for hours with other members of Engine 216 and Ladder 108 who had come to the site on their own. I told him that a fireboat was supplying us, that we were supplying Engine 207. He said he was going to follow the three-and-a-half-inch line and talk to the chauffeur of Engine 207. I told him I'd join him. I handed him the flashlight and Senilla tool. I handed him the radio. Ed Schollmeir was on duty now.

Chapter 16

NIGHTFALL

LIEUTENANT ED Schollmeir followed the three and a half-inch hose line toward Engine 207 while I walked beside him. It wound over and under other hose and over and around large pieces of steel and through the dust and through the water that was pooling everywhere. Engine Company 207 was still parked where it had been, but the supply line from Engine 216 was no longer hooked up to it. Engine 207 had run out of fuel and was replaced by a spare pumper brought in from the shops. The supply line from Engine 216 was now connected to the spare pumper. The spare pumper supplied the siamese connection for 90 West Street and supplied a hand line stretched up Washington Street toward the pile. The chauffeur from Engine 207, Steve Ferriolo, was still operating the pumps. Ed Schollmeir introduced himself to Steve and explained that he was now in command of Engine 216. The chauffeur nodded and continued to monitor the pumps on the spare rig.

As we made our way back, we looked up at 90 West Street. Smoke poured from several windows on three or four floors—two near the roof and one or two in the middle—maybe around the tenth floor. Steam and water blew out of some of the windows. The firefighters were making progress, putting out fire, trying to save the building. Smoke pushed from multiple locations throughout the collapse, all over the pile. To the north, Seven World Trade Center was gone. Large industrial light towers were being set up as the first hint of twilight began to settle on the site. Fire crews were constantly arriving, moving quickly, determined to go to work. We got back to Engine 216.

Front-end loaders and large tow trucks were picking cars up off South End Avenue and moving them south. The street was being cleared for the heavy equipment and supplies that would start to be assembled soon. Firefighters from Engine 216 and Ladder 108 gathered near the rig, they were despondent, dejected. Ted Murray and John Johnson stood nearby with Lieutenant Schollmeir. I was off duty now. My boots cut into the back of my ankles so I made my way to an ambulance and pulled off the boots and the EMTs gave me some Band-Aids for my feet. They wanted to do more. Everyone did. I put the boots back on and walked to a bar-restaurant on the northwest corner of South End Avenue and Albany Street.

Firefighters sat at the outdoor tables, dust-covered, exhausted. A large tray of muffins had been set out and I picked one up and blew off the dust and took a bite. I chewed deliberately and forced myself to swallow. I realized it was the first thing I'd eaten since the morning, but I wasn't hungry. I threw the muffin into a plastic garbage bag just inside the restaurant. I made my way toward the back, passing firefighters who sat in small groups, their helmets and coats lying across the tables. Firefighters carry at least one spare flashlight, and I used mine to find the bathroom in the back. The water had been off all day and the stench was strong. I made my way back onto the street.

Normally at large scale operations, once the situation is stabilized, as firefighters run across friends they haven't seen in a while there are greetings and stories, some catching up with one another. But this time, the entire scene was devoid of joy; there was only silence and sadness and shock. No smiles. No stories or polite inquiries about family. The information being exchanged was very specific, and very solemn. "Was Gregg working today?" "Have you seen Gerry?" "Where was the last place you saw Frank?" It was unlike anything any of us had ever experienced before.

I wandered north, slipped past some companies waiting to be assigned and past chiefs trying to keep control of the operation. I looked out onto the utter and complete devastation in the deepening darkness, and was chilled down to my very soul. I made my way back onto the pile, using the flashlight once again, trying to search. I searched over and under the steel, looking and listening, hoping to find some movement, some life. I passed an engine company pouring water on a fire raging unseen within the rubble; the smoke was tough to take. I crawled and climbed and lost track of time and at some point the search felt aimless, inadequate. I began to make my way slowly off the pile. I searched as I went, but I knew I was done. My feet were bad, my lungs filled with dust and my eyes scratched and raw.

I made my way back to Engine Company 216 and retrieved the shoes I had placed in the cab when we got the response ticket to Two World Trade Center. I walked east to West Street, past the Command Post, past the fresh troops still arriving, past the tower ladders that were pouring water into 90 West Street. I passed Engine 207 and zigzagged north and east around the destruction, each block at first filled with papers and dust and steel, but then slowly clearing. The collapse site was illuminated and the blocks immediately surrounding the site were filled with police cars and ambulances with their emergency lights flashing and their headlights glaring. Occasionally I passed an FDNY pumper, all the hose stretched off of it, all the tools and fittings gone. The fire department vehicles that I now passed didn't have their lights on; they were dark and empty. It got darker and darker two and three and four blocks away, and the streets grew quiet.

I passed a group of police officers; they greeted me warmly. They were with some National Guard troops, all of them standing in the dust. I wasn't sure where I was going and my head was pounding. I passed an army Humvee and a New York State trooper car, their occupants talking quietly, the glow of a cigarette making the group appear almost ordinary. But in the darkness I felt completely alone and totally numb. I thought about Danny Suhr and began to cry for the first time—to really cry. Yet I knew that because he had died, the rest of Engine 216 lived. And his death also saved the members of Engine 205, who had stopped to help. Danny also saved the members of Engine 217, except for Firefighter Steve Coakley and Firefighter Neil Leavey who tragically lost their lives in the collapse. We had all been heading into the lobby of the south tower. No one in the south tower survived.

I limped out into City Hall Park; it was black and deserted. And then I saw a light at the far end of the park. The light was coming from the entrance to a subway station and I walked slowly toward it and saw that it was the Number 6 train, the train that could get me home. I climbed down the stairs, walked through the emergency exit door that was propped open and stood on the nearly empty platform. It was cold in the station, cold and brightly lit. Water dripped from somewhere, but other than that it was quiet. I took off my turnout coat and folded it over and put it on a bench and put my helmet on top of it. I removed the suspenders of my bunker pants, pushed them down and stepped out of the pants and boots. I stood on the platform in my wet socks then put my feet carefully into my shoes. I heard the clicking, switching sound that precedes an approaching subway train and stale air rushed into the station and I picked up the coat and bunker gear and helmet as the train car screeched to a halt. I got on and sat heavily on a hard plastic seat.

The train lurched into motion and I tried to close my eyes, but I kept seeing Danny Suhr when I did. And I saw West Street and Chief Barbara and Seven World Trade Center. My eyelids scraped my eyes anyway; they were too scratched to close. I looked at the empty seat across from me, and only slowly became aware that the other passengers on the train, although few and spread out, were all looking at me. I glanced at each of them and then looked down at the turnout coat and helmet laying across my lap, at the bunker pants and boots on the floor.

"Are you all right?" asked a passenger who sat across from me and to the right. He was a large man, in his late thirties or early forties.

"I lost one of my guys. A jumper hit him as we headed into the south tower. We put him in an ambulance. He saved our lives." I said it without thinking, the words just came out. The large man just barely shook his head; his eyes grew glassy. A young man sitting a few seats down from him put his hand over his mouth and a woman on the same side as me blew her nose in a fistful of Kleenex. The train jerked as it gained speed and soon we all sat in the increasing noise of the accelerating subway, alone, together, sharing the unspeakable tragedy of the day.

Chapter 17

HOME

I GOT home and walked down the driveway alongside my house. Light came through the large kitchen window, through the curtains, soft and diffused, and the light just barely illuminated the driveway. I carried the bunker gear straight to the backyard to leave it in the garage. I walked as quietly as I could, not wanting to disturb the silence, to disrupt the peace. Then Mary appeared at the back door. The light from the kitchen poured out of the doorway around her, and it was bright and it flooded the grass and the garage and the driveway. Mary was backlit, in silhouette, and now I acknowledged for the first time that I hadn't really been sure that I would ever see her again. The realization was physical, a blow, it made me catch my breath. I was afraid to blink, afraid she might disappear. I dropped the gear as she came down the stairs and we walked quickly toward one another and then embraced. We wrapped our arms around each other, and I closed my eyes, and I finally exhaled.

Our children began to appear at the back door. They ran down the stairs and over to us. We cried. It felt too good to be true—to be back home. I finally drew back a bit, and Mary and I looked at each other, and she tried to smile but I could see the apprehension and the concern. She would tell me years later that she felt sick to her stomach, sick with worry, that I was covered in dust, that each eye lash was coated. She said, "You look exhausted."

"Are you okay?" I asked. But it was a nonsensical question, just words, and I continued. "I'm going to put my gear in the garage. I'll be right in."

Eileen, Kathryn, Margaret and Paul sensed the gravity of the moment, the enormity of it, the lack of clarity, and they reached out once more, a little tentative now, a touch, a kiss, and then headed back to the house—up the stairs, through the door, into the kitchen—and the door closed behind them. Mary waited while I hung the gear in the garage and then we hugged once more in the darkened backyard, silent, as close as we could get.

My family was navigating unchartered waters. We were thrilled to see each other, of course, but we all knew that everything had changed. When we had left the house that morning, Mary and I for work, our children for school, we didn't know what was about to happen. Nobody did. Eileen and Kathryn were at St. Francis Prep, a senior and a junior. Eileen had a friend whose father was in the FDNY, Lieutenant Ken Phelan; she asked Eileen if she had heard anything, if I was okay. And when school reopened on Friday of that week, Eileen asked the same friend if her father was all right, and the girl responded that he was still missing. Kathryn had answered the phone when I called and knew something was wrong. She knew that I did not call from work, and could never call from the scene of a fire. Margaret and Paul were twins, in eighth grade at Holy Family School. One of Margaret's teachers, Mrs. Nunez, asked if I was working, as if just making conversation, and when Margaret said yes, Mrs. Nunez couldn't respond, she was silent. She nodded and turned and left the room. Paul wondered what was happening, why the younger kids were being picked up by their parents, why the TV was on in the main office, why the teachers were talking in hushed tones.

And now we were returning to a different world. The same scene was taking place all over New York City, all across America. Was it okay to eat? To talk about anything other than those who were lost or trapped or missing, those who had died? Was it all right to go to sleep?

The firefighters and police officers and EMTs who lived through the collapse, who were working at Ground Zero, were more like soldiers than typical first responders. When soldiers leave the battlefield, sweating and dirty and disoriented, they usually return to some sort of base or bunker or camp, to a group of fellow combatants who are in the same place physically and mentally and emotionally. They lived through something awful, not all of them survived, and they have a tacit understanding that they won't ever forget what they just experienced, and who they experienced it with. Maybe there's some oblique mention of how bad it was, and maybe not; they know they may be called upon to do it again. There might be some gallows humor, some blowing off of steam, some crude coping mechanisms at play. Conversely, Home is that place of comfort somewhere far away, a concept, almost theoretical, the past and the future, the place that is peaceful and hopeful and safe. But now firefighters and police officers and emergency medical technicians were in the battle of their lives all day and were returning home at night. And Home wasn't immunized from the conflict. Families were also involved, assaulted all day by the images on TV, touched by the closeness of the loss, physically exposed to the smoke and the dust.

In the past when firefighters had a close call or a difficult fire, they got home and didn't talk about it. They didn't want to, didn't have to. But this wasn't like that. There was no denying it. Families looked to each other for assurance that things were going to be all right. But were they? Was anything ever going to be all right again? And what about the men and women who weren't coming home? What about the husbands and wives, the mothers and fathers, the sons and daughters, the sisters and brothers, the friends and neighbors who left for work in the morning and didn't come back? What about the families that already knew that their loved ones had died? And what about the thousands and thousands of families who still hadn't heard anything? They just didn't know.

I stood in the kitchen and tried to remember what it was that my children needed, tried to remember how to act, but all I could see was the site, and the desolation. They probably sensed it, and Mary knew it, and she kept the conversation going, and finally they started to make their way upstairs. Mary and I planned on heading back to the firehouse, to pick up my car, but first I took a shower. I was crushed by the guilt of being alive, being home, surrounded by love. I didn't even know the name of Danny's widow, didn't know the name of his daughter, but I knew they wouldn't find any comfort that night. I felt I should have been the one to die. Yet at the same time I was incredibly grateful to be alive. It was the ultimate contradiction, yet no contradiction at all. I stood in the shower and tried to let the hot water blast the dust off, tried to open my eyes, to rinse them out, and inhaled the steam to try to clean out my lungs. But nothing was working.

Mary and I drove to the firehouse. She put her life on hold, put everything else aside and put me first, for days, for months, for years. We went to funerals together, to memorials, to wakes, she took care of our children, our home; she took care of me. We got to the firehouse after midnight and a lot of firefighters were still there. I really didn't know most of them by name, but everyone I met was incredibly welcoming. They embraced me like I was a member of their family. We hugged and exchanged expressions of sorrow and shock. No one knew how many had died, but it was obvious that the number would be unbearably high. And the loss of Danny was heart-wrenching.

The FDNY had instituted a twenty-four hour on, twenty-four hour off system, an 'A' Group and a 'B' Group. I was in the 'B' Group, due in the next day at 7:00 AM. Mary and I left in separate cars. When we got home, we sat at the kitchen table and drank a cup of tea. We held hands across the table and shared the tragedy of the day. We couldn't believe I would be leaving in a few hours to go back to work. We couldn't believe that both buildings had collapsed and so many must have died. We couldn't believe I had survived. We headed upstairs and lay down. I stared at the ceiling, at the blinds, at the walls. I couldn't close my eyes because they were too scratched, and when I did, I kept seeing Danny Suhr and the dust and the devastation. I wanted to get up and go back down to the site, to look for God knows how many who were missing, but I was too tired to move. At some point I fell asleep. I woke at first light, and we poured cups of coffee and sat once more at the kitchen table in the quiet of the dawn. Finally, I stood up to leave, and we hugged once again—standing motionless in the kitchen in each other's arms. Neither of us wanted to let go.

• • •

Ted Murray's tour ended at 6:00 PM. He had been on duty for twenty-four hours but remained at the site several more hours. When he finally left, he was told that there was a boat, a Boston Whaler, tied up alongside the fireboat, and that it would give him a ride back to Brooklyn. He walked to the river, got on the fireboat and climbed down to the deck of the Boston Whaler along with a few other firefighters. The boat headed south through New York Harbor, around the tip of Manhattan and north up to the Brooklyn Navy Yard. From there they got a ride back to the firehouse. It was around 11:00 PM when he got back. He couldn't see too well, his eyes were badly scratched, so he found an ambulance and they flushed them out thoroughly. He still couldn't see very well but he and Tony Sanseviro went across the street to a bar and had a beer, the same bar where the retirement party was held the night before, except the night before seemed like years ago now.

Engine Company 216's rig was still at the site pumping. John Johnson said that he and the other members of Engine 216 were ordered to operate a hose line from the Marriot Hotel into 90 West Street. He remembers that the hose was already in place and that they were on a high floor and they were able to get water through the windows on to the upper floors of 90 West Street and extinguish some fire. Officially his tour wouldn't end until 9:00 AM, but several times members of the firehouse offered to relieve him, encouraged him to leave, to head back to the firehouse. Yet as confused and shocked as he was at the events of the day, one thing he was certain of was that he wanted to stay with the rig until it left the scene. He felt like it was something that he had to do. Engine Company 216 got released at around 4:00 AM and John Johnson and the others pulled back into the firehouse and began to prepare the rig to get it back in service.

• • •

Nancy was still at Jackie's house as it started to get late in the afternoon. She wanted to go home. She wanted to regroup, to keep moving—she didn't know what else to do. Briana wanted to stay, to keep playing, but Nancy took her by the hand and they went home. An hour or so later the doorbell rang; it was her brother Neil. He was devastated. They stood alongside one another in the kitchen, staring straight ahead in silence. He eventually asked, "What do we do now?"

"I don't know," Nancy answered. There was no road map to follow. They didn't know what the future held, how they would continue. Danny's parents, Ed and Sheila, were still in Oregon. All flights were grounded; they couldn't get home. Once it began to grow dark, Chris Suhr came over. He remembers Nancy giving Briana a bath and the two-year old splashing her legs in the shallow water in the tub and calling out, "I want my Daddy...I want my Daddy *now*."

Brian Charles and Kenny Collins came over, besides being firefighters with Danny, they were family friends. Nancy's parents were there. Her father, Louis, took it especially hard. He thought of Danny as a son. Nancy said, "My father would sometimes repeat a story, like fathers do sometimes. And Danny would listen politely every time. And laugh every time." Danny had worked with Louis cleaning out sewers those two summers, they enjoyed each other's company, they liked each other, were close. They loved each other.

The long night wore on for Nancy—unreal, a blur. The shock of the planes flying into the buildings; the Twin Towers collapsing; the empty streets in Manhattan; the dust and the papers and the silence; the trauma teams at Bellevue; the firefighters and friends despondent and guilt ridden; the unknown numbers missing and lost; the constant sound of sirens; it all served as a tragic backdrop to the cold hard fact that Danny was gone.

On September 10, 2001, the night before Briana would start pre-school, Nancy and Danny had finally gotten their daughter to sleep in her own bed. It felt like the right time to do it. On the night of September 11th, as Briana grew sleepy, Nancy picked her up and carried her into the bedroom that she had shared with Danny and placed the child gently in their bed. Nancy lay awake and cried quietly. She barely slept at all, but Briana slept peacefully next to her mother that night. And they would sleep together every night, mother and daughter, side by side, until Briana turned twelve.

Chapter 18
WEDNESDAY 9-12-01

ON WEDNESDAY September 12, Danny's brother Chris wondered how his parents would get home from Oregon. No one knew when the airspace would reopen, and when it did, how long it might take to get on a flight. So he reached out to the Uniformed Firefighters Association, and spoke to Matty James, the UFA Brooklyn Trustee. Matty had been close to Danny. He said he would get in touch with some contacts at Delta Airlines and told Chris to stay by the phone.

Chris waited less than an hour and received a call from a supervisor at Delta who told him not to worry, that his parents would get home. The supervisor knew Dan and Chris from N&D Pizza and wanted to do anything he could to help. In a short time another representative called and it turned out that he had gone to James Madison High School with Danny, he knew him well, and was distraught that he had died. He took down Sheila and Ed's information and promised that they would be flying as soon as possible.

By Thursday night the FAA lifted the ground stop in the United States and Ed and Sheila boarded one of the first flights heading east. They landed in Atlanta and then took a flight to MacArthur Airport on Long Island and were picked up by friends and taken to their home in Brooklyn. They arrived Friday morning to face the unthinkable, the loss of their son. They shared their grief with their family and friends and neighbors, and with firefighters Ed had worked with. They tried to comfort one another, for the loss everyone faced, tried to find solace, leaned on each other, all of it heart breaking. But at least they were home. And nearly twenty years later Chris Suhr was still incredibly thankful to Matty James, the UFA, Delta Airlines and all those who helped get his parents back as quickly as possible during those first dark days.

· · ·

Everyone was taking a beating, but the company commanders were especially crushed. Company commanders were directly responsible for everything that happened in their company. With so much going on in so many firehouses, they couldn't count on too much help. Captain Ted Jankowski, Captain Jim Gormley, and Captain Paul Mannix were three such Company Commanders.

Ted Jankowski saw the image on TV of the first plane striking the north tower, and he immediately called Danny Suhr and then rushed into the firehouse. When he found out that Danny was injured, he instructed Firefighter Brian Charles to pick up Nancy Suhr and bring her to the hospital. He knew it would be difficult for Brian to take care of it, and he knew Brian would do it well. Captain Jankowski went to Bellevue and made sure he was there before Nancy arrived. He determined that Tony Sanseviro and Chris Barry were in no shape to operate safely after what they had been through, so he ordered them back to the firehouse. He reached out to counselors at the hospital so that they would be available for Nancy, for the other members of Danny's family, and for Tony and Chris. Later that night he would tell Ted Murray to get his eyes checked by a doctor, to get them taken care of and to let them heal. And in the subsequent weeks he told all his firefighters that the FDNY Counseling Unit might help.

Engine Company 216 remained at the site pumping for nearly eighteen hours. When they finally got back to the firehouse, Jankowski had to make sure the rig was still serviceable, that it hadn't been damaged. He had to ensure that they had the proper equipment to get ready to respond to fires again in Williamsburg. But he also had to make sure it was properly staffed, that the firefighters who were grieving the death of Danny were able to operate. He had to make sure that Nancy had whatever she needed to help her get through the night, and then the next day and the day after that. He had to help plan and coordinate a line-of-duty funeral. Long term, he had to make sure that Nancy and Danny's family would be cared for, taken care of indefinitely. At the same time, he was dealing with his own personal grief, with the loss of Danny and so many other friends and fellow firefighters. Like everyone else, as the days went by, he was spending hours and hours at Ground Zero. And somehow, he had to convince his family that he could stay safe doing it all...

I saw Captain Jim Gormley on Wednesday morning at the Winter Garden. The Winter Garden was being used as a staging area, where maybe a 100 firefighters now waited for orders. I sat with five firefighters who had been assigned to me at the quarters of Engine Company 211, the mustering site established for north Brooklyn. They were stragglers in need of an officer, and I was a covering captain in need of firefighters, so we were paired together and sent to Ground Zero on a bus with 30 or 40 other firefighters. The roof of the Winter Garden was heavily damaged and shards of glass—some quite large—hung at severe angles from above. The metal framework was twisted and hanging free. It seemed like an incredibly unsafe place for firefighters to gather, but then again, everything is relative. It was a lot safer than The Pile, the place all the firefighters were waiting to get out on.

Jim Gormley was my lifelong friend; we met when our mothers pushed us in strollers alongside each other in Stuyvesant Town on the

Lower East Side of Manhattan. His father had been in the FDNY and now Jim had nearly twenty-five years on the job. He was the captain of Engine Company 40 in Hell's Kitchen. He was leading his company past the tables and chairs where the firefighters sat waiting for an assignment, and he was walking toward the opening out onto the pile. I stood as he approached; we shook hands, and then hugged each other. Jim said, "Good to see you." And we nodded our heads in agreement; it was good to see each other. Alive.

I said to him, "I lost Daniel Suhr. I was in Two-Sixteen, we were heading into the south tower, a jumper hit him. He saved our lives. We put him in the ambulance and the building collapsed." The words came out of me like water down a hill.

"I'm so sorry, Pablo." He used a nickname I hadn't heard in a long time.

"I'm sorry too," I said. And I motioned at the destruction around us. "It's unbelievable."

"We won't know what it all means for 20 years," he said. "We're going to need some historical perspective."

"Are your guys all right?"

"They're still working. We're looking for them now," he said. His firefighters gathered around their captain as he spoke. I didn't know it at the time but every member of his company who had responded the day before was missing. And every member of Ladder 35, the truck company in his firehouse, was missing. His whole battalion, Battalion 9, was missing. It was too much to grasp. "They're awaiting relief. We're going to find them, get them home," he said. In the FDNY, a firefighter is considered to be awaiting relief when they're still at work, still at a fire, even though their normal tour of duty has ended. He spoke with clarity and conviction, eyes locked on mine. He touched my shoulder, like a blessing. "Stay strong."

Jim Gormley's father, Hubert, retired after serving 42 years in the FDNY; he rose to the rank of Assistant Chief, the Borough Commander of Staten Island. Before the twin towers were built Hugh Gormley advised us to go down to the Lower West Side of Manhattan, to see the area before it was demolished. He told us that the area was known as Radio Row and it was unique and shouldn't be missed. So in the summer of 1966 we rode our bikes, two ten-year-old's, down to Radio Row.

Now Jim Gormley led the firefighters from Engine Company 40 out of the Winter Garden and a short time later my company was also given an assignment out on the Pile, but I didn't see him again that day. We didn't see each other for nearly a year. He and the members of Engine Company 40 and Ladder Company 35 and all the units in Battalion 9 searched until the site was finally shut down in May of 2002. Like so many others, they never found any survivors, and they didn't find the remains of many of their members. Prior to this, when a firefighter died in a fire, the FDNY stopped, the entire city paused, a funeral would be held and thousands and thousands of firefighters from all across the nation would attend. Individual companies had memorials each year marking the anniversary of any line-of-duty death in their firehouse. If more than one firefighter died, such as when six firefighters were killed at the Waldbaum's Fire on August 2, 1978 or when twelve firefighters were lost in the 23rd Street Collapse on October 17, 1966, all firefighters knew the dates, knew the circumstances of the fires. The idea that we may have lost an entire battalion, three engine companies, two ladder companies, a rescue company, a battalion chief and his aide, was inconceivable...

Captain Paul Mannix was the Company Commander of Engine 207 in downtown Brooklyn. On Wednesday night Engine 207 was still operating at the site and at around 11:00 PM I was ordered to Engine 207's firehouse. I was to be the officer for an engine company from New Jersey that was filling in for Engine 207. There were three additional units in the firehouse on Tillary Street, Ladder Company

110, Battalion 31 and Division 11. It was one of the largest firehouses in the department. I spent some time describing FDNY procedures to the firefighters from New Jersey and realized we needed a couple of very basic items in order to operate at all. The 11th Division Commander, Deputy Chief Philip Burns, approached us on the apparatus floor and told me to let him know if we needed anything. I let him know we needed two radios, three roll ups of 2 ½ inch hose with a nozzle, and a Custodian hydrant wrench. Within minutes a firefighter assigned to the firehouse appeared with the requested items.

I stood on the apparatus floor in front of the engine at around 2:00 AM on Thursday morning and looked out through the open overhead doors. I looked west and south, past the Manhattan Bridge, toward Ground Zero in the distance. The smoke pouring from the site was lit from ground level by the floodlights and it looked for a moment like a massive ghost rising from the tip of Manhattan. It was so large it had a certain mass; it looked permanent. A van pulled up and members of Engine 207 and Ladder 110 climbed out. They were slow and stiff and dejected. Captain Paul Mannix was among them and he walked toward me. We shook hands and he asked, "What do they have you doing?"

"I'm the officer for an Engine from Jersey. I guess 207 is still pumping? I saw it on West and Liberty, after the collapse. The chauffeur was by himself."

"Steve was the chauffeur. Everyone else is missing. He's pretty torn up," he said. The officer of Engine 207 on September 11th was Lieutenant Ken Phelan. He was actually assigned to Engine Company 217 but was working in 207 for the day. The three firefighters that the chauffeur responded with that day, Shawn Powell, Kevin Reilly and Karl Joseph, had left the rig with their roll ups and spare cylinders while the chauffeur hooked up to a hydrant. They followed Lieutenant Phelan towards the towers and Steve never saw them again. As the days and weeks passed it became clear that many firefighters had suffered a similar fate, sole survivors.

"How long have you been down there?" I asked.

"All day. We're going to wash up, head back in the morning," he said. He shook his head slightly. He looked tired but determined. He was looking for his guys, and like so many other firefighters, it was personal. He wasn't going to stop until he found them.

"God bless, Paul. Stay safe," I said. He walked off towards the stairs in the back, slowly, with a slight limp. The company commanders were searching at the site, then going back to their firehouses and piecing their companies back together. They were trying to get rigs, hose, masks, radios, tools, so that they could respond and protect their neighborhoods. They were taking care of the families of the missing firefighters and soon enough were planning funerals and memorials. The firefighters in every firehouse on the job worked day and night to take care of everything, to take care of everyone, working more hours than they ever had before, making sure nothing was overlooked, no matter how big, no matter how small. It was an impossible task, but somehow they were doing it, and they would keep doing it for months.

The engine company from New Jersey was sent back sometime after 6:00 AM and I left the firehouse at 7:00. I drove east on the Brooklyn Queens Expressway, back toward Queens, toward home. I would become the Company Commander of Engine 207 a few years later, and would take the same route many times, but that morning the road was empty. My eyes were beginning to heal; they were still scratched, but not as raw. I think the tears helped. I looked to my left as I drove, toward Manhattan, and the buildings sticking up into the sky looked incredibly vulnerable, defenseless, like targets. They looked jagged, exposed, arrogant. Or maybe innocent. Old fashioned. They looked like they were built in ancient times, some distant epoch, before any of this could have been imagined.

Chapter 19
ST EDMUNDS

ON THURSDAY September 13, Captain Ted Jankowski was at the site with three of the firefighters who had worked on September 11, Tony Sanseviro, Chris Barry and John Johnson. The fourth, Ted Murray, wasn't with them because the Captain didn't want him to go until his eyes healed, but Ted went down anyway, on his own, with a couple of friends who were firefighters in Long Beach. The captain and the others searched alongside several members of Engine 216 and Ladder 108, searching for hours until they found a deceased victim late in the afternoon. Firefighters from every firehouse in the city were there. Everyone was searching for survivors. Thousands of people were unaccounted for, missing, and there was the very real hope that there were voids, pockets where people were gathered, they might have water, might be protected by a quirk of how the steel fell, they might be safe. They would be found and removed and returned to their families. The site was being sectioned into quadrants, and search patterns were being implemented. What no one knew at the time was that the last survivor had already been rescued, on the day before, at around 1:30 in the afternoon. So, the search for life went on for weeks.

Telephones rang in countless homes, questions couldn't be asked, answers couldn't be given. Ordinary people were improvising, adapting to extraordinary circumstances. Words were being invented by the hour; Ground Zero; the New Normal; Missing Persons Posters; The Pier; The Pile; Portraits of Grief. Phone numbers were established for those looking for information, but there wasn't a whole lot of information to disseminate. The sidewalks were empty and the streets were deserted. Schools were closed, the New York Stock Exchange wouldn't reopen until the following Monday. Nonessential personnel were encouraged to stay home, and the security zone isolating Lower Manhattan was expanded ever northward; first no one could get south of Chambers Street, then Canal Street, Houston Street, 14th Street.

Supplies were pouring into the site: backhoes and grapplers and dump trucks; light towers and generators; hard hats and gloves and gallons of water. Plans were made, then changed, and changed again. City agencies and private firms were just beginning to determine how many might be missing: the Fire Department; the New York Police Department; the Port Authority of New York; Cantor Fitzgerald and Lehman Brothers; Windows on the World. And what about the visitors? Who could account for those who decided just that morning to go to the observation deck on the 107th floor of the south tower? For those making deliveries to the massive buildings? Those popping into the office of a brother, a sister, a friend?

Firefighters don't normally seek assistance, but the Counseling Services Unit, the CSU, was overwhelmed. The FDNY CSU had been established in the 1960's and was expanded in the 1980's to deal with particularly difficult fires and emergencies, with marital problems, alcohol and substance abuse, the death of loved ones, and all the same problems faced by any large organization. Peer Counselors were created in 1990 after the Fire Department responded to the Happy Land Social Club Fire where 87 civilians perished. But after September 11th the responsibilities of the CSU expanded exponentially. Suddenly the CSU was called upon to serve hundreds of firefighters who were trying to process the loss and destruction. Folding tables and portable chairs were set up in storage areas in the offices of the CSU to turn them into treatment rooms. Psychologists and professional counselors eventually volunteered their services. Family Liaisons were invented; firefighters from individual firehouses that took it upon themselves to be the point of contact between headquarters and the loved ones of their missing members. It was a constant creation of solutions to problems that never existed before, it was a constant sense of catching up.

· · ·

Nancy took Briana to her first day of preschool on Thursday when the school reopened. As they approached the entrance Nancy saw the other parents, smiling and teary eyed, sending their little ones off on their own for the first time. She wished she hadn't come. Nancy kissed Briana good-bye, and her daughter skipped off, barely looking back, which was good, and bad. As Nancy was walking back to her car she saw a familiar face, Marty Charles, the brother of Brian. He had just dropped off his child and he approached Nancy and asked, "Is there anything I can do?" He was serious and sincere. He wanted Nancy to know that she wasn't alone, that he, like many others, was there for her if she needed it.

Nancy looked up at him and said, "Can you bring him back?" Marty had a physical reaction to her words, his face fell, he grew pale and looked down at the street. He obviously felt terrible, and so did she. Nancy instantly regretted it. She said, "I learned a lesson at that moment. This was bigger than me, bigger than any one person. People cared. They cared deeply, about everyone who was lost, and they cared about me, especially when they saw Briana. They loved her, were really distraught, really wanted to help, in any way they could." And standing in the street on her daughter's first day of school, two days after Danny's death, she determined never to do that again.

By Friday the family was gathering and they planned a wake for the next two days followed by a funeral mass on Monday. Nancy described how back in June, during the wake for Harry Ford, she and Danny had sat quietly in the funeral home paying their respects. At one point Danny leaned over, speaking close to her ear, and said that if it ever happened to him, he didn't want a picture of their daughter holding his fire helmet on the front cover of the New York newspapers the next day. And Nancy, maybe in trying to lighten the mood, said that he would need to find a very large place for the wake because he had so many friends. Danny said to have it at the Marine Park Funeral Home. At the time Nancy had no idea that she would be carrying out his wishes less than three months later.

• • •

On Saturday September 15, the first three funerals were held for members of the FDNY. Chief of Department Peter Ganci, First Deputy Commissioner William Feehan and the Fire Department chaplain, Father Mychal Judge, were laid to rest. It would be the first of many days, especially Saturdays, when more than one funeral mass would be held. On one Saturday in October 22 separate memorials and funerals were held.

Chief Peter Ganci and First Deputy Commissioner William Feehan were at the command post on West Street across from One World Trade Center, shortly before it collapsed. They were ordering members out of the building and sending everyone north, away from the area. William Feehan had held every position possible in the FDNY and Peter Ganci was the highest-ranking uniformed member of the department; they possessed an incredible wealth of knowledge and experience. Father Mychal Judge had responded when the first plane struck the first tower. He positioned himself in the lobby of the north tower with his firefighters, lending support and praying for all, the firefighters; the poor souls on the planes; those above the point of impact. These three leaders were with their beloved department to the very end.

• • •

The wake for Danny Suhr was held at the Marine Park Funeral Home on Saturday and Sunday. Chris Suhr was surprised at how many people told him stories about Dan, about how kind and thoughtful he was, how much it meant to them that Dan had taken the time to smile at them, to include them, to make them feel loved. Of course, Chris saw it all while growing up, he knew all about it, but he was still surprised at the number of people who sought him out to tell him their story. They told Chris what he already knew, that his brother Dan was an extraordinary man.

The funeral mass was held on Monday September 17, at St. Edmunds Roman Catholic Church on Ocean Avenue in Brooklyn, the same church where Danny and Nancy were married twelve years prior. Captain Jankowski arranged the mass. He said, "So many members of the firehouse made it happen, especially Doug Adams, Brian Charles, Kenny Collins, Glen Tracy—and the retirees. Without the retirees it wouldn't have worked." They crowded into the church, took the place of the thousands of active firefighters who just couldn't be there, and as a result, the church was packed, overflowing with firefighters, family, and friends, many standing in the aisles down the sides and in the back.

At the end of the mass there were several eulogies. Dan's brother-in-law Mike spoke, and Deputy Chief Philip Burns and Captain Ted Jankowski. Pudgy Walsh also spoke. "Danny was one of the best human beings I've met in my time on this earth," Pudgy said. His words, as always, were from the heart, his eyes angry and filled with tears, his face flushed red as he almost lost his voice. He captured the raw emotion of the moment, looking out at the congregation, and down at Nancy from the pulpit. "The most complete player I coached in 54 years of coaching the Mariners. He was a great friend. A great firefighter. A devoted husband, a loving father. Danny Suhr was a huge loss to this city."

A large, framed photograph of Danny sat at the front of the church and when the mass ended and the family began to leave Nancy was handed the picture of her husband. She clutched it against herself as she walked down the aisle. She had not taken Briana to the mass. She was trying to honor Danny's wish that his daughter would not appear on the front cover of the newspapers if he ever died in the line of duty. When she was about to exit the front doors of the church, Brian Charles noticed that Nancy held the picture faced away from all those lined up in the street outside. He told her and she turned it around so that everyone could see Danny's smile one last time. The picture of Nancy holding the photo of her husband at the entrance doors of St Edmunds Roman Catholic Church appeared in the *New York Daily News* the next day.

Chapter 20

THE BLESSING OF THE STONE

AFTER THE funeral mass, Danny Suhr was laid to rest in St Charles Cemetery in East Farmingdale on Long Island. Six months later, on Saturday April 6, 2002, his family and friends gathered for the Blessing of the Stone. The fires at Ground Zero had finally been extinguished, The Pile was now known as The Pit, and the Fire Department had settled into a grim routine. Firefighters were detailed for one month at a time, a day shift and a night shift. They searched for the remains of the missing, working with the operating engineers and the ironworkers; the heavy equipment operators and steel workers; eventually searching 1.4 million tons of material. Everything that was recovered was carefully combed three times before being removed to the Fresh Kills landfill on Staten Island. There the debris would be sifted three more times in an effort to ensure that nothing, however small, would be missed.

There were large numbers of individuals and groups working together at the site, representatives from countless professions and trades. Security was paramount. The NYPD and Port Authority Police, the National Guard and New York State Troopers, the Secret Service and the FBI were among those ensuring the safety of everyone working at Ground Zero. Urban Search and Rescue Teams from all across America rotated through and gave their invaluable assistance. The Department of Sanitation played a crucial role, hauling debris, constantly restoring the streets of lower Manhattan and operating the Staten Island landfill. City, State and Federal agencies coordinated the activities that impacted the infrastructure and navigated the political obstacles necessary to keep the work proceeding. Private engineering firms provided essential expertise; they were constantly consulted as to the safety and structural integrity of the heavily damaged buildings throughout the area.

The Southwest Incident Management Team (IMT), sanctioned by the US Forest Service, helped organize the entire effort. The IMTs were incredibly effective in managing large-scale, long-lasting events, such as forest fires in the western United States. The Southwest IMT had the unique experience and knowledge that was required to provide overall coordination. They demonstrated the necessary flexibility to meet the constantly expanding challenges of the numerous entities operating in close proximity at the sprawling site. The FDNY did not have an Incident Management Team at the time, but in the years to come it would develop its own highly effective IMT.

The generosity of the human spirit was on display everywhere, from early in the afternoon on September 11th, when cases of bottled water first appeared at Ground Zero and buckets for the bucket brigades arrived from Home Depot; to the next days and weeks when work clothing was available, coveralls, pants, jackets, and gloves; to the Red Cross and the Salvation Army establishing semi-permanent operations until the site was shut down. The volunteers were ubiquitous, grief counselors; doctors and nurses; religious; physical therapists; chiropractors; accountants and lawyers; psychologists; massage therapists; and people from all over the world offering whatever help they could.

That terrible day led to months and months of selfless acts of kindness and sacrifice, New Yorkers helping New Yorkers; residents in Washington DC helping one another; the good people from Shanksville, Pennsylvania opening their homes to the loved ones of those who died on Flight 93; firefighters from throughout the nation traveling to New York to attend firefighter funerals because members of the FDNY couldn't possibly make it to all of them. By the time World Trade Center site was officially closed on May 30, 2002 it's estimated that over 500,000 individuals worked in the rescue and recovery effort.

The total number of people killed at the World Trade Center was 2,749. The final toll, including those lost at the Pentagon and in the field outside of Shanksville, Pennsylvania was 2,996. It would be the highest ever for an attack on American soil. Yet over 17,000 were safely evacuated from the twin towers before they collapsed, the greatest single rescue operation in our nation's history.

Nancy Suhr was still at the very beginning of adjusting to life without Danny. On April 6 she stood in St. Charles Cemetery with her parents and with Danny's parents, with their brothers and sisters, firefighters and friends. It was a crisp day, in the upper thirties, with a stiff wind out of the north. The clouds were low and they raced across the sky and the sun appeared intermittently through the breaks in the clouds causing bright light, then shadow, to fall on the cemetery. Near the end of the service the group stood before the grave and the priest extended his hands over the headstone and said the blessing. He then turned to face those standing in front of him. He made the sign of the cross and all those gathered blessed themselves in the name of the Father and the Son and the Holy Spirit. And then it began to snow.

The snow fell in large flakes, dry and cold. It fell into their faces and onto their coats and it whipped across the grounds on the gusty breeze. The falling snow filled the air and Nancy and the others looked at one another and looked at the snow as it fell. Soon the visibility was reduced and for a moment everything seemed to disappear except for the immediate vicinity of Daniel's burial place. Nancy took it as a sign. An unmistakable sign from her husband that he was there; that he was all right; that she was going to be all right.

· · ·

Father Mychal Judge was the Chaplain for the Fire Department of New York. The New York City Medical Examiner gave him the official designation of Victim #0001, the first recorded death at the World Trade Center. Father Mychal Judge was a Franciscan priest at St. Francis of Assisi Church on West 31st Street near Seventh Avenue in Manhattan. He was beloved by countless New Yorkers, the homeless and the hungry who he served on the St. Francis breadline each morning at 6:00 AM; the family members of firefighters as he held their hands and prayed with them in hospital rooms and funeral homes; the rich and powerful of New York City, leaders in finance and government and business; his parishioners at St. Francis Church; and the countless AIDS patients he served from early in the 1980's when the crisis first began until his very last days. His work habits were legendary and his devotion to God and his fellow human were a living testament to the love of Jesus Christ on earth.

The symbolism of Father Mychal Judge as the first to perish, leading the way, forging the path, the good shepherd guiding his flock, is powerful. The image is comforting; Father Mychal Judge taking care of all those innocent victims on airplanes and in offices, lives snuffed out in an instant, and the FDNY Chaplain opening his arms wide, calling out to his firefighters as they climbed up the stairs of the towers, like Jacobs Ladder, encouraging them to climb higher still, heavenward. It's not a great leap to imagine him meeting Daniel Suhr early on, and for Daniel, smiling and caring, offering to give Father Mychal Judge a hand. Daniel Suhr standing beside him, reaching down, helping the firefighters up the last few steps to their eternal rest and reward—Daniel Suhr saving firefighters as he departed this life and assisting firefighters into the next.

· · ·

When Nancy and I sat down together for a conversation on April 2, 2019 the first thing she told me was that this would have been her 30th Wedding Anniversary. She said that at first she was going to reach out to tell me that she couldn't meet on that date. But then she realized that actually it was the perfect day to meet; she would love to spend a few hours talking about Danny, about their lives together, and about the years without him.

She said that since Danny died it was hard trying to make all the decisions on her own, especially concerning Briana. "I've often second-guessed myself," she said. She and Danny wanted a child very much, and it took years until Briana was born. As Danny lay on the gurney in Bellevue Hospital on September 11th Nancy promised that their daughter would know him. From the earliest stages of dealing with the loss of her husband, Nancy felt a laser-like focus and crystal-clear purpose; she would do everything in her power to give Briana the absolute best life that she possibly could. Briana gave Nancy a reason to live, a reason not to dwell on her own grief and pain. From the very first moments, Nancy told Briana about her father, the good and the bad.

Of course, raising a child as a single mother presented multiple challenges, both large and small. In the fall of 2004, when Briana was six, she got appendicitis and Nancy reached out to her sister Luanne and her mother-in-law Sheila and they rushed her to Schneider's Children's Hospital, where she was operated on the next day. Afterward Briana lay in her hospital bed calling out for her mother, but they wouldn't let Nancy in. The doctor said that Briana's veins were collapsing, they were doing their best, but there was still a lot of fluid in the abdominal cavity. Nancy told the doctor, "You have to keep her alive. She *can't* die."

Briana was finally stabilized and they let Nancy into her room. Briana had to stay in the hospital for over a week and Nancy never left her side, sleeping, eating, spending every minute with her. One day the doctor came into the room and, with tears in his eyes, said, "I didn't know you lost your husband on September 11th. I'm so sorry. If I had known I don't know if I could have operated." This is the way it was for Nancy, the public side of the personal loss.

This was also how it was for so many of those who lost loved ones that day, for the nearly 3,000 families coping with the sudden, heart-wrenching personal loss, along with the communal loss, the shared grief. Victims from every part of America were killed that day, and from over 90 nations throughout the world. The loss was unprecedented, but the good that was coming out of it was also unprecedented. There was the sense that we were all in this together, that the attacks wouldn't take away our humanity, that we were going to continue living, and more than that, we weren't going to become like the terrorists, we were going to treat each other with love and respect. This was all a part of it too.

Just as raising Briana without her husband presented Nancy with unique problems, it also provided countless rewards. Nancy and Danny enjoyed what their daughter did and said from the very first, and Nancy has continued to appreciate and delight in her daughter ever since. Briana has been a source of incredible comfort and joy, and maybe even more so since Danny was taken from them. Nancy gets to see Danny in Briana; in the way she carries herself, her kindness to others, her positive outlook, her courage.

Danny was difficult to say no to. Once he had an idea, a plan, he was hard to resist. His enthusiasm and energy were contagious—his self-confidence, his faith in his fellow human beings. He felt empathy for others, a deep natural concern and compassion. As Nancy said, "I have more compassion now. I don't think I had it when Danny was alive, but *he* did."

Daniel Suhr died that day, but he also lived that day. He lived as he always lived—focused, determined, concerned with those around him. Nancy and Briana always feel his absence, at times missing him by the hour, by the minute; missing his love, his presence. But they also live with the knowledge that his life, his death, saved others. This does not, of course, replace him, nothing can do that, and grief doesn't end, it doesn't stop, but it can evolve, and hopefully, on some days, that knowledge helps.

September 11th is like a wall separating two different worlds, pre and post, before and after, a borderline between life and death, impenetrable, unforgettable. Countless people were forever changed that day, in New York, across America, and all over the world. They all have a story. There are thousands of stories, each deeply personal and meaningful, each as valid as the next. This is one story. Daniel Suhr died, and his death saved the lives of thirteen firefighters. We can never repay him. We might try to thank him, we might try to thank Nancy and Briana and all those who love him, for their sacrifice, for their loss. But it would always fall short. Maybe all we can do is remember, and tell the story.

Daniel Suhr stopped us from entering the south tower, stopped us from certain death. This story is a tribute, a story to be shared, a story that needs to be told, that cannot be forgotten. This is Daniel Suhr: a story of September 11th.

ACKNOWLEDGEMENTS

I WOULD like to thank the firefighters working on September 11th in Engine Company 216: Tony Sanseviro; Ted Murray; Chris Barry; and John Johnson. You were extremely generous and selfless in being willing to sit down and share your memories. You helped ensure that the final version of this story be as accurate as possible. Thank you.

I would also like to thank the following members of the FDNY who read this book before it was complete, who encouraged me to continue in the effort, and who offered invaluable guidance: Brian Charles; Brian Easerly; Ted Jankowski; Tim Keenan; Jack Kleehaas: Danny Williams; Gerry Wren; my brother-in-law Paul Geoghegan; and my lifelong friend Jim Gormley. I'd especially like to thank Frank Leeb for his close reading, thoughtful suggestions, professional guidance, and mostly for his kind words.

I would like to thank Andrew Serra. He whole heartedly embraced this project from when I first described it to him in the Spring of 2019. He edited the book with the understanding and appreciation that only a fellow firefighter could bring, and with the professionalism and expertise that only an accomplished author could provide. In addition, he helped me navigate my way through the complex process of publication. Thank you.

I would like to thank Glen Edelstein for his professionalism and talent, for laying out, formatting, and designing the book, inside and out, and for turning the manuscript into the finished product. Thank you. I would also like to thank my friend since childhood, Stephen Downes. As soon as he learned what the book was about, he came up with the concept for the cover; it seemed effortless, like it always existed, like it had to be. Thank you.

I would like to especially thank Daniel's family. Chris Suhr has been understanding throughout this entire process. Reliving those days was difficult for him, yet he did so to help move this project forward. Thank you for your trust, your good humor, your kindness, and for keeping it real. And, of course, to Nancy Suhr; thank you. Thank you for embracing this undertaking from the first moment it was proposed, thank you for sharing painful, personal memories of your life with Daniel, and thank you for exhibiting such remarkable strength in the face of your heart-breaking loss. I would also like to thank Briana, I know she was and continues to be a great comfort to you in all ways, big and small.

I would like to thank my brothers and sister: James; Gerry; and Chris; and my brothers-in-law and sisters-in-law: Virginia; Kathryn; Daniel; Anne; and Paul. Anne served proudly as a Court Officer in lower Manhattan during and after September 11th. Thank you all for showing me what family is. Also, to the members of our family who we lost too soon, Patricia and Matthew, you are greatly missed.

I would also like to thank the friends I've known all my life: Timothy Brosnan; Mark Curley; Terrance Doyle; Chris Fleming; Gerard Long; Chris Sheldon; Brian Sullivan; Jim Wolfe; Stephen Downes and Jim Gormley. We are all better persons for having known each other. And for those who have passed on: Bobby Fulham; Kelly Grant; Kevin Gleason; and Tommy Ross—you live on in our hearts.

I'd like to thank my daughters and son, Eileen, Kathryn, Margaret, and Paul, for their courage in the face of the horrific events of September 11th. Like so many others, you couldn't have known where to place such an unprecedented experience, but I witnessed firsthand your grace and acceptance and love. In addition, I'd like to thank Paul for reading early drafts and offering excellent insights. Thank you.

Most of all, I'd like to thank Mary, my wife, for her love and encouragement, for her inspiration, and for being my first reader. Thank you for supporting me as I traveled to do interviews, or spent time doing research. Thank you for reading several drafts and offering invaluable advice as to the proper direction that the book should take, and for keeping me on the right path. As with everything else that is good in my life, I owe you a debt of gratitude. This project truly could not have been completed without the love of my life; thank you Mary.

I'd like to thank the FDNY Counseling Services Unit, the CSU. Firefighters don't normally ask for help, yet after September 11th firefighters from all over the city reached out and the CSU answered the call. They geared up almost overnight, storage rooms were converted to treatment rooms, folding tables and metal chairs were set up, retired members came back to assist, and eventually psychologists and counselors from across America volunteered their services. The CSU did an outstanding job and continues to do excellent work every day, thank you.

Firefighting is based on teamwork. All firefighters start out knowing very little about the job, then they learn from those who came before them. I would like to thank and acknowledge all those dedicated and exceptional professionals who I had the pleasure and the honor to work with through the years, especially the members of the companies in the firehouses where I was assigned: Engine 76 and Ladder 22 on West 100 Street in Manhattan; Engine 84 and Ladder 34 in Washington Heights; Engine 95 and Ladder 36 in the Inwood section of Manhattan; Engine 207 and Ladder 110 in downtown Brooklyn; and Engine 287, Ladder 136 and Battalion 46 in Elmhurst, Queens. You are the best of the best, and I will always remember our years together with great love and respect, with fondness and joy. Stay Safe.

Finally, 'last but not least,' I would like to thank you, dear reader. Thank you for contributing to the cause, as all the proceeds will be donated to charity. Thank you for the time and energy that you have committed to this book, and most of all, thank you for sharing this story with us, for becoming a part of it. By joining us on this journey, you have paid tribute to Daniel Suhr and to all those lost on September 11th, to those we are losing still, and to the loved ones who have been left behind. On behalf of all of us involved, Thank You.

Paul Conlon
July 2021

NOTES

Chapter 1   **Monday September 17, 2001**

7 *The World Trade Center had an unusual design, basically a tube within a tube: Why Did the World Trade Center Collapse? Science, Engineering, and Speculation* by Thomas W. Eagar and Christopher Musso JOM, 53 (12) (2001), pp. 8-11

9 *Each building weighed over 500,000 tons*: ibid.

10 *No one had been found since Wednesday at 1:30 PM when Genelle Guzman-McMillan was rescued*: New York Magazine Aug 27, 2011 *Survivor, Last Pulled Out* by Matthew Shaer.

Chapter 2   **Homecrest**

12 *Chris Suhr said that all his father did was work, and that he was never the same after Daniel's death:* interview with Chris Suhr on March 22, 2019.

12 *High school can be a tough place, but Dan would always take the time to stop and smile and say hello, especially to the kids who felt left out:* interview with Chris Suhr on March 22, 2019

13 *Chris related a story about one of Dan's first days at the College in the Desert*: interview with Chris Suhr on March 22, 2019

14 *Daniel Suhr first asked Nancy Lanzetta out on March 2, 1978 when she was in seventh grade at St. Edmund's Elementary School and he was in the eighth grade*: interview with Nancy Suhr on April 2, 2019

15 *Danny loved becoming a firefighter, was absolutely ecstatic, overjoyed*: interview with Nancy Suhr on April 2, 2019

16 *His brother Ed had graduated from West Point in June of 1984 and got in a nearly fatal car accident three months later, in September*: interview with Chris Suhr on March 22, 2019.

Chapter 4 **Impact**

25 *In the 1960's Radio Row was a vibrant neighborhood:* "World Trade Center: The History of the Old Radio Row," from the website: National Public Radio, Inc.

25 *The sidewalks were crowded with people searching for the particular part*: Photograph by Berenice Abbott "Radio Row, 1936"

26 *The first store on Radio Row had opened in the early 1920's and over the next forty years hundreds of businesses became part of this thriving community:* "The History of "Radio Row," NYC's First Electronics District" from the website: gothamist.com

30 *As I sat in the kitchen John Johnson, the proby, was checking the rig*: interview with John Johnson 3-6-19.

31 *Chris Barry recalled that Daniel Suhr walked into the kitchen rolling up the sleeves of his dark blue FDNY work shirt*: from interview with Chris Barry on 2-18-19.

Chapter 5 **Assigned**

34 *After the plane flew into the north tower, Daniel Suhr told the others that they needed to double check the tools and equipment*: from interview with Ted Murray on 2-15-19.

34 *John Johnson answered the phone when the captain called*: interview with John Johnson on March 6, 2019

34 *When they were done with the rig Daniel Suhr asked Ted Murray if he wanted to drive*: interview with Ted Murray on 2-15-19.

Chapter 6 **Response**

41 *Chris Barry told me that he and John Johnson, sitting on the right side of the rig that was heading south, had a good view of the twin towers*: interview with Chris Barry 2-18-19

41 *Tony Sanseviro said that Daniel Suhr was talking, telling him, among other things, that this was going to be a really bad fire, and Tony was a little anxious to hear him talking like that*: interview with Tony Sanseviro on March 14, 2019

44 *Chris Barry remembered NYPD police officers warning us away so that we wouldn't step on something in the street; it may have been a body*: interview with Chris Barry 2-18-19

44 *Two Engine Companies were just behind the chief, Engine 205 and Engine 217:*

The members working in E205 on September 11, 2001:

Lt Hays, FF Tom Boccarossa, FF Christopher Patrick Murray, FF George Clancy, FF Timothy Julian (L118)

The members working in E217 on September 11, 2001:

Lt Tommy McGoff, FF Tom Michelle, FF Danny Moran, FF Jimmy Hart, FF Steve Coakley (RIP), FF Neil Leavey (RIP)

46 *Chris Barry heard Danny say*: interview with Chris Barry 2-18-19

Chapter 7 **Belle Harbor**

47 *Nancy and Danny grew up in working class homes, good homes, but Danny wanted them to have more*: interview with Nancy Suhr on April 2, 2019

48 *Nancy said that he had that effect on people, that he made people around him believe: interview with Na*ncy Suhr on April 2, 2019

48 *Chris described those years simply, "Dan was the boss, I was the horse."*: interview with Chris Suhr on 3-22-19

50 *John Johnson was also working that day and he remembers Daniel standing in the middle of the kitchen, crying*: interview with John Johnson on March 6, 2019

Chapter 10 **The North Tower**

69 *John Johnson would later describe that when the second collapse began he ducked into a building on West Street*: interview with John Johnson March 6, 2019

Chapter 12 **The Hospital**

83 *Emergency vehicles were converging on the area, two thousand NYPD and Port Authority police officers, more than 100 EMS ambulances plus dozens of private ambulances, over two hundred FDNY units*: The Encyclopedia of 911: First Responses

84 *The ambulance pulled up at the emergency entrance of Bellevue Hospital and Chris Barry described a crowd of men and women standing and waiting*: interview with Chris Barry on 2-18-19

85 *Nancy Suhr was in the butcher shop with her two-year-old daughter, Brianna, when the first plane struck the first tower*: interview with Nancy Suhr on April 2, 2019

86 *Nancy said that Brian Charles never used the air conditioning in his old car*: interview with Nancy Suhr on April 2, 2019

87 *When he left the bank he saw smoke rising over the southern tip of Manhattan and he turned on the radio in his car and heard that two planes had crashed into the World Trade Center*: interview with Chris Suhr on March 22, 2019

89 *Chris Barry remembers when Nancy Suhr arrived at the hospital. He couldn't face her, could barely look her in the eye*: interview with Chris Barry on 2-18-19

90 *When Nancy saw Chris he was standing against a wall on the far side of the room and his face was gray, ashen*: interview with Nancy Suhr on April 2, 2019

91 *Eighteen years later as she related the story, she still regretted not spending more time with him in the hospital*: interview with Nancy Suhr on April 2, 2019

91 *When they stepped out of the squad car there were a lot of firefighters gathered there*: interview with Chris Barry on 2-18-19

92 *"He's in heaven with God," Nancy said. The words came out simply, without hesitation*: interview with Nancy Suhr on April 2, 2019

Chapter 17 **Home**

123 *When he finally left, he was told that there was a boat, a Boston Whaler, tied up alongside the fireboat, and that it would give him a ride back to Brooklyn*: interview with Ted Murray on 2-15-19.

124 *John Johnson said that he the other members of Engine 216 were ordered to operate a hose line from the upper floors of the Marriot Hotel into 90 West Street*: interview with John Johnson on March 6, 2019

125 *He remembers Nancy giving Brianna a bath and the two-year old splashing her legs in the shallow water in the tub and calling out, "I want my Daddy...I want my Daddy now"*: interview with Chris Suhr on March 22, 2019

127 *So he reached out to the labor union that represented firefighters in the FDNY, the Uniformed Firefighters Association, and spoke to Mattie James, the Brooklyn Trustee*: interview with Chris Suhr on March 22, 2019

127 *And nearly twenty years later Chris Suhr was still incredibly thankful to Mattie James and the UFA and Delta Airlines and all who helped get his parents back as quickly as possible during those first dark days*: interview with Chris Suhr on March 22, 2019

128 *Later that night he would tell Ted Murray to get his eyes checked by a doctor, to get them taken care of and to let them heal*: interview with Ted Murray on 2-15-19

128 *And after a few weeks he told Chris Barry that the FDNY Counseling Unit might help*: interview with Chris Barry on 2-18-19

131 *He and the members of Engine Company 40 and Ladder Company 35 and all the units in Battalion 9 searched until the site was finally shut down in May of 2002*: In Our Tears by James Gormley

The following members from Engine 40 and Ladder
35 were killed on 911:

Engine Company 40, Lieutenant John Ginley; FF Bruce Gary;
FF Steve Mercado; FF Kevin Bracken; FF Mike Lynch (on rotation
from Ladder 32); FF Mike D'Auria (Probationary FF
14 week training program)
Ladder Company 35: Captain Frank Callahan; FF Jim Giberson;

FF Mike Otten; FF Mike Roberts; FF John Marshall (Engine 23);
FF Vinny Morello

Chapter 19 **St Edmunds**

137 *She said that she learned a lesson at that moment; this was bigger than her, bigger than any one person*: interview with Nancy Suhr on April 2, 2019

137 *Nancy described how back in June, during the wake for Harry Ford, she and Danny sat quietly in the funeral home paying their respects*: interview with Nancy Suhr on April 2, 2019

139 *Of course, Chris saw it all while growing up, he knew all about it, but he was still surprised at the number of people who sought him out to tell him their story*: interview with Chris Suhr on March 22, 2019

139 *"Danny was one of the best human beings I've met in my time on this earth," Pudgy Walsh said as he concluded*: website: todayremember.blogspot.com *Bracelets For America Remembers* FF Daniel "Danny" Suhr, FDNY Tuesday June 14, 2011. Pudgy Walsh gave an incredible eulogy at the funeral mass for Daniel Suhr. This quote was taken from the above referenced website. He may have said it at the funeral or at a football game honoring Danny some years later. But these were his words and this was his sentiment so I took the liberty to include them at this point in the story -PC

Chapter 20 **The Blessing of the Stone**

143 *Nancy took it as a sign. An unmistakable sign from her husband that he was there; that he was all right; that she was going to be all right; all of them: interview with Nancy Suhr on April 2, 2019*

144 *When Nancy and I sat down together for a conversation on April 2, 2019 the first thing she told me was that this would have been her 30th Wedding Anniversary*: interview with Nancy Suhr on April 2, 2019

145 *From the earliest stages of dealing with the loss of her husband, Nancy felt a laser like focus and crystal clear purpose; she would do everything in her power to give Brianna the absolute best life that she possibly could*: interview with Nancy Suhr on April 2, 2019

145 *In the fall of 2004, when Brianna was six, she got appendicitis*: interview with Nancy Suhr on April 2, 2019

146 *Danny was difficult to say no to. Once he had an idea, a plan, he was hard to resist:* interview with Nancy Suhr on April 2, 2019

BIBLIOGRAPHY

BOOKS

Brown, Michael Everett. *What Brothers Do,* Texas, Virtualbookworm. com, 2019

Daly, Michael. *The Book of Mychal: The Surprising Life and Heroic Death of Father Mychal Judge*, New York, St. Martins Press, 2009.

Dwyer, Jim and Flynn, Kevin. *102 Minutes: The Untold Story of the Fight to Survive Inside the Twin Towers*, New York, Henry Holt and Company, 2005.

Ford, Michael. *Father Mychal Judge*, Mahwah, NJ, Paulist Press, 2002.

Gormley, James. *In Our Tears*, New York, James Gormley, 2012.

Langewiesche, William. *American Ground: Unbuilding the World Trade Center*, New York, North Point Press, 2002.

Serra, Andrew. *Finding John*, New York, Tudor City Press, 2018.

Smith, Dennis. *Report from Ground Zero*, New York, Penguin Group, Plume, 2002

REFERENCES

Kean, Thomas H, and Lee Hamilton. *The 9/11 Commission Report: Final Report of the National Commission on Terrorist Attacks Upon the United States*. Washington, D.C.: National Commission on Terrorist Attacks upon the United States, 2004. Print.

Lawson, J. Randall and Vettori, Robert L. *NIST Federal Building and Fire Safety Investigation of the World Trade Center Disaster*, Washington DC, US Government Printing Office, 2005.

FROM THE 911 COMMISSION REPORT:

McKinsey & Company, "FDNY Report," August 19, 2002 FDNY report "Report from the Chief of Department, Anthony Fusco," in Manning, ed., *The World Trade Center Bombing*, p. 11

INTERNET ARTICLES

Bazant, Zdenek P. and Murphy, Walter P. "Why Did The World Trade Center Collapse?" *civil.northwestern.edu*, SIAM News Volume 34, Number 8

Eagar, Thomas W. and Musso, Christopher. "The World Trade Center Had an Unusual Design: Why Did the World Trade Center Collapse?" *tms.org*, Journal of the Minerals, Metals & Materials Society, 12/2001

Flood, Joe. "The Encyclopedia of 911. First Responses."

Nymag.com. August 27, 2011

Izenberg, Jerry. "The Story of 911's First Hero, Football and Colin Kaepernick." The Star Ledger. New Jersey Real-Time Sports. *nj.com*

Kern, Jonathan. Yonkers, Francis. Schneck, Ed. Lanset, Andy. Brody, Morton. "World Trade Center: The History of Old Radio Row." *National Public Radio, Inc*, Fox Movietone Newsreel June 3, 2005

Simon, Jordan. "Radio Row: NYC's First Electronics District." *gothamist.com* in Arts and Entertainment July 26, 2016

Young, Michelle. "Radio Row: A tinkerer's paradise and makers space, lost to the World Trade Center." *6sqft.com*, September 25, 2017

"The Story of New Amsterdam." The New Amsterdam History-Center. *Newamsterdamhistorycenter.org*

PHOTOGRAPHY AND FILM

Radio Row

Photograph:Berenice Abbott's well-known photograph, Radio Row, was taken in 1936 on Cortlandt Street.

Film:Fox Movietone News Outtakes from the *Moving Image Resource Collection* at the University of South Carolina Copyright 2018 Richard Boylan

FDNY Oral Histories (as published by the New York Times)

FDNY Procedural Manuals (2001)

Engine Company Operations

Ladder Company Operations Ladders 1-6

Multiple Dwellings

Communications Manual

Training Bulletins: Mask

Regulations

INTERVIEWS

Nancy Suhr on April 2, 2019

Lieutenant Edward (Ted) Murray on February 15, 2019

Captain Christopher Barry (E290) on February 18, 2019

Firefighter John Johnson (E302) on March 6, 2019

Firefighter Tony Sanseviro (E216) on March 14, 2019

Firefighter Chris Suhr (E280) on March 22, 2019

Deputy Chief Ted Jankowski on April 7, 2021

FDNY GLOSSARY
Terms in Use On September 11, 2001

Alarm: when the public calls for help the FDNY responds. The response of the FDNY to the public is considered the first Alarm. Then, if more resources are needed, the fire officer in charge at the scene will transmit additional alarms; Second Alarm, Third Alarm, Fourth Alarm, ect...

Alarm Assignment: the FDNY Dispatcher sends the resources deemed appropriate by the information given by the public. For instance, one Engine Company is dispatched for a medical emergency, one Ladder Company for a stuck elevator. For structural fires, up to three Engines, two Ladders, one Rescue Company, and a Battalion Chief are sent. Each additional alarm requires the response of four Engine Companies, two Ladder Companies, and various special Units. The Chief in Charge of each alarm is as follows: Second Alarm, a Deputy Chief; Third Alarm, the Citywide Tour Commander; Fourth Alarm, the Chief of Operations; Fifth Alarm and above, the Chief of Department.

Apparatus: any fire department vehicle.

Assignment: each firefighter is given a particular job to do, a position, or assignment. In the Engine Company, in addition to the Officer, firefighters have one of five positions, ECC (Engine Company Chauffeur), Nozzle, Back-Up, Door, and Control. In Ladder Companies the positions are, Officer, LCC (Ladder Company Chauffeur), Outside Vent, Roof, Forcible Entry, and Can. Assignment also refers to the particular duties given to a Unit at a fire or emergency.

Building Inspection: all buildings in NYC, except one and two-family private dwellings, are inspected by the FDNY for fire safety.

Citywide Tour Commander: a Staff Chief in charge of all activities in the department outside of normal business hours. They notify the Chief of Department of unusual incidents. They are the Chief in Charge of a third alarm, although they can respond to any incident they deem appropriate.

Command Channel: the chief in charge of a large-scale operation may institute a separate channel to use to communicate with other chief officers. A channel distinct from the tactical channel.

Company Commander: Captains charged with the administrative duties and responsibilities in their respective units (paraphrased from *Regulations* Page 1-1)

Committee Work: routine maintenance carried out each day by the firefighters in the firehouse.

Company Drill: each tour every Company sets aside a period of time for teaching, training and practicing any and all firefighting procedures.

Company Journal: a 500-page 14 x 11 inch bound book that is maintained on the housewatch. In it are recorded everything that occurs in the firehouse each day. The firefighter on watch records all activities in black pen. Lieutenants, Captains and Chief Officers take notations in red ink. The company journal is required to be stored for twenty years. In actuality, many firehouses have company journals dating back decades.

Custodian Hydrant Wrench: a special wrench with a magnet designed to open up hydrants that are equipped with a magnetic clutch. The hydrants that they are used on are known as Custodian Hydrants. They were developed to help stop neighborhood children from freely opening hydrants, especially during the summer, sometimes reducing water pressure to dangerously low levels.

Deck Gun/ Deck Pipe: aka Akron "New Yorker" deckpipe or "Stang" nozzle. It is permanently affixed to the top of the Engine, supplied directly by a 3" pipe from the pumps capable of delivering water in excess of 300 gallons per minute. The large volume of water can be used for a quick knockdown of a large body of fire such as a store fire or lumberyard or to protect civilians trying to use a fire escape to get out of a burning tenement. (FFP Engine Company Operations Page 11-2)

Department Radio: the radio on each fire department apparatus that allows communication with the dispatcher. It is supplied with a handset for speaking and listening. In addition, speakers are mounted on the rig so that all firefighters are able to hear messages from the dispatcher. The Department Radio has the ability to be set to one of six frequencies, one for each of the five boroughs of NYC and the 'citywide' frequency. Sometimes called the rig radio.

Engine / Fire Engine: the fire department apparatus that has pumps and carries hose of various sizes. Engine Companies provide water and stretch hose lines to the fire area and extinguish the fire. Members of the Engines also respond to CFR/D or medical emergencies and perform life-saving first aid.

Facepiece: the clear polycarbonate covering for the face that allows air to be supplied to the firefighter when wearing an SCBA in an IDLH. It also provides some thermal protection to the face.

Field Communications Unit: also known as Field Comm. It is a Fire Department apparatus dedicated to communications at large-scale incidents and staffed by dispatchers, and a fire officer who is in charge. Field Comm is dispatched on Second Alarms and above. Once on the scene all communications between the incident and the central communications office go through this unit.

First Due: Battalion chief, Engine or Ladder assigned to arrive first at an alarm box. (*Regulations* Page 1-2)

Ground Zero: the term commonly used to refer to the World Trade Center site.

Group: the FDNY utilizes a 25-group chart with all members assigned a group number, 1-25.

Halligan: a high carbon content steel hand tool designed by Chief Hugh Halligan in 1948 that combined multiple tools in one. It has a fork at one end and an adz and pike at the other end. It can be used in countless ways to help force open doors, windows, gates, and most other obstructions that firefighters might encounter that are otherwise impeding their access to the fire area.

Handie-Talkie/ HT: a portable radio carried by each firefighter to allow them to communicate with one another. On September 11, 2001 all officers carried Handie-Talkies, but not all firefighters were assigned HT's yet. They would be within the year.

High-Rise Building: in NYC any building over seventy-five feet tall. A High-Rise requires certain fire protection features, including a standpipe and fire protected construction.

Hood: firefighters wear a hood around their neck and pull it up over their head, over the mesh of the SCBA face piece and beneath their helmet, before entering a fire area. It offers thermal protection to the ears and neck.

Hose Fittings: essentially plumbing fittings that allow the connection of numerous combinations of hose and other hydraulic devices, such as nozzles, reducers, increasers, gates, wye's, manifolds and outlets.

Housewatch: a designated area, usually enclosed, on the apparatus floor at the front of the firehouse. It serves as the place where alarms are received and from which the fire companies are notified of a response. It is also where all interactions with the public are coordinated. A firefighter is always on watch. Each housewatch has a minimum of the following, a phone; a computer terminal for receiving alarms; a bell or a buzzer to alert the Companies that they have a response, an intercom for communicating with all spaces in the firehouse, a desk and a chair. The company journal is maintained in the housewatch.

Hydrant Pump: A handheld pump with a small length of hose attached used to pump standing water out of the barrel of a hydrant. When hydrants leak during the winter, if the water is not manually pumped out, it can freeze and render the hydrant inoperable.

IDLH: an acronym for Immediately Dangerous to Life or Health. An atmosphere that is contaminated by the products of combustion.

Irons: the ax and the halligan, aka forcible entry tools. They are carried by the Forcible Entry firefighter in the Truck Company whose responsibility is to gain entry to the fire area.

Knockdown: an expression to indicate that the main body of fire has been extinguished, or 'knocked down', but that final extinguishment has not yet occurred.

Ladder Company: aka Truck Company. The fire department apparatus that carries ladders and has multiple types of tools for use at a fire or emergency. At a fire, members of the Truck Company locate the fire and provide entry and access into the fire area so the Engine Company can extinguish the fire. The Truck Company searches for trapped people and rescues and removes them. They also mitigate multiple hazards including gas leaks, water leaks, stuck elevators, steam leaks and yes, even the occasional cat stuck in a tree. The FDNY has Tower Ladders and Aerial Ladders. The Aerial Ladders are one of two types, the Rear Mount or the Tiller.

Line: in the FDNY a hose is called a line, short for hoseline or handline. Hose comes in various diameters, 1 ¾ inch, 2 ½ inch, 3 ½ inch, and 5 inch. Firefighting demands flexibility, but each size hose has some generally accepted uses. "The 1 ¾ handline is the primary attack line used at structure fires." The 2 ½" hose is used for "an advanced fire on arrival...when a large volume of water is required...for a purely defensive position... for a large body of fire"...for fires of unknown size and "all hose lines stretched from standpipes." The 3 ½ hose is used to supply standpipes and for inline pumping and relays and the 5" hose is used by fireboats and satellite units to supple water long distances. (Source: FFP Engine Company Operations)

Manifold: a portable hydraulic device for distributing water at large-scale operations. It consists of one 3 ½" inlet and six 2 ½" outlets. Up to six hose lines can be supplied by the manifold, and it can be positioned close to the area where it is needed, thereby reducing the amount of hose needed for the individual lines.

Mask: aka SCBA. It is the device that provides air to the firefighter while operating in an IDLH.

Mayday: a message transmitted over the handie-talkie at the scene of a fire or emergency to alert the Incident Commander to a situation that requires immediate action. It is only given in one of the following five circumstances:
A structural collapse is imminent
A structural collapse has occurred
A firefighter is unconscious or has suffered a life-threatening injury
A firefighter is missing
A firefighter (including the firefighter giving the mayday) is lost or trapped Once a mayday is given, all radio transmissions are to cease while the IC responds to and addresses the mayday. (FDNY Communications Manual Section 9.4.1)
Members: The term "members" indicates uniformed members of all

ranks and grades. (*Regulations* Page 1-2)

Military Time: ...employs the 24 hour clock and when written or spoken always uses four digits. (*Regulations* Page 1-2)

Portable Radio: Handie-Talkie.

Projects: one type of High-Rise Fireproof Multiple Dwelling. They were built as low-income housing and are often operated by the New York City Housing Authority.

Pumper: another name for an Engine Company

Put to work/work: a general expression to mean that a Fire Company has been given a certain task to accomplish at an operation, or that they are engaged in that task.

Purge Valve: a valve on the side of mask facepiece that allows the firefighter to control the flow of air into the facepiece.

Quarters: Any fire station or department building wherein fire apparatus is housed and members are assigned for duty. (*Regulations* Page 1-2)

Radio Code Signal: aka "10-codes." A series of numbers from 10-1 (call your quarters) to 10-99 (unit will be operating for at least 30 minutes) to facilitate radio communications. They are used for clarity and brevity and are known by all members of the department.

Rank: the FDNY is a "quasi-military" organization. It has a strict chain of command made up of members of several ranks. The ranks, each requiring success on a civil service exam, are Firefighter, Lieutenant, Captain, Battalion Chief, and Deputy Chief. The Fire Commissioner appoints Staff Chiefs from the rank of Deputy Chief.

Regulations: a book listing all the rules and regulations of the uniformed force. A copy shall be issued to every uniformed member of the Department, for which the member shall be held strictly accountable. (*Regulations*: Introduction)

Relocated: the movement of a Fire Company into another firehouse when an area is depleted of fire coverage.

Response Area: aka Response District: When used in conjunction with a battalion or Company shall mean the area to which they are assigned to respond on first alarms.

Riding List (BF-4): a two-inch by four-inch form used to record all firefighters working each tour in each Company. It has the name, assignment, riding position and group number of each member on the rig. The form also records the Company number, date and tour across the top. It is made out in duplicate, with one copy on the rig, and one copy in the possession of the officer in charge at all times. If the firefighters need to be accounted for at an operation, the BF-4 on the rig can be consulted to see who is working. The Riding List is also a black board or white board mounted on the wall of the firehouse near the Company that it serves. On it is recorded the same information as the BF-4. It is updated each tour.

Rig: aka apparatus

Roll Call: at the beginning of each tour the officer in charge of a Fire Company gathers the firefighters to give out assignments and discuss any and all information pertinent to the Company for that particular tour. The "roll call" is also a term used to describe the information that the officer records in the company journal at the beginning of each tour. An officer is said to "write the roll call." Aka '0900 entries' or '1800 entries.'

Roll Ups: a fifty foot length of 2 ½" hose folded and held by straps to be carried by a firefighter into a fire in a High-Rise building. Three roll ups are normally stored on an Engine Company, providing approximately 150 feet of hose line to extinguish the fire.

Rotation: Probationary firefighters were moved out of their assigned Company within their first three years on the job. They were normally sent to two different types, an Engine and Ladder Company.

Run (response): when a Company is assigned to a fire or emergency.

SCBA: Self Contained Breathing Apparatus aka the Mask, worn by firefighters in a contaminated environment to provide approximately 30 minutes of air. It consists of a face piece, hose, frame and air cylinder

Scott Air Cylinder: aka cylinder or air cylinder. The tank filled with compressed air and carried on the back as part of the SCBA to provide breathing air to firefighters.

Senilla Tool: small hand-held pry bar carried by officers.

Senior Firefighter: an expression to describe that a particular member has a lot of time on the job. The "senior man" was used to describe the firefighter with the most time in a particular Company.

SOP: Standard Operating Procedures.

Special Units: any special piece of apparatus designated to perform specific duties. (*Regulations* Page 1-3)

Standpipe Kit: used for fires in high-rise buildings consisting of a minimum of the following; a nozzle, hand control wheel for outlet valve, in-line pressure gauge, pipe wrench, spanner wrenches and door chocks. In addition, special adapters may be required. (FFP Engine Company Operations Section 9.4.1)

Standpipe System: piping that runs from the basement to the top floor of a high-rise building. Also, dependent on the height and area of the structure and accessibility for fire department vehicles, other structures also require standpipe systems such as parking garages or bridges. There is a siamese connection on the exterior of the building at street level to allow the attachment of a 3 ½" supply hose line and it has 2 ½" outlets, in the stairway or hallway, on each floor to allow firefighters to connect a hose line and extinguish fire. (FFP Engine Company Operations Section 9.1)

Tactical channel: aka Primary Tactical Channel, normally Channel 1. It is the Handie-Talkie channel used by all members at an operation. If necessary, the chief in charge may institute a Command Channel, and even secondary tactical channels, if the incident is large enough.

Tenement: multiple dwelling in New York City consisting of Old
Law Tenements (built prior to 4/12/1901) New Law Tenements
(built on or after 4/12/1901 and before 4/18/1929) and Class "A"
Non-fireproof multiple dwellings (built on or after 4/18/1929),
eventually known as Apartment Houses. They were the most
common residential type of building in the city for many years,
and therefore, they were the type of dwelling in which most fires
occurred, the "bread and butter" of the FDNY. (FFP Multiple
Dwelling Fires Page 1)

The Pile: a term that members of the FDNY and others used to
describe the vast debris field left behind after the destruction of
the World Trade Center. The Pile was painstakingly searched for
the remains of all those lost. After some months, as more and
more material was removed, and the mountain of debris began to
get lower and lower, the site became known as The Pit.

The Pit: a term that members of the FDNY and others used to
describe the vast debris field left behind after the destruction of
the World Trade Center. Just as with The Pile, The Pit was painstakingly searched for the remains of all those lost. On May 30,
2002, no more material was left and there was no longer any possibility of finding the remains and the search was officially ended.

Three Way Gate: aka a Wye, a device used to distribute water
remotely from an Engine Company, consisting of one 2 ½" inlet
and two 1 ¾" outlets

Truck Company: aka Ladder Company.
Twenty-four (as in 24 hour mutual): the FDNY is staffed based